Feminism and the Politics of Resilience

T0375006

Feminism and the Politics of Resilience

Essays on Gender, Media and the End of Welfare

Angela McRobbie

polity

First published in 2020 by Polity Press
2

Polity Press
65 Bridge Street
Cambridge CB2 1UR, UK

Polity Press
101 Station Landing
Suite 300
Medford, MA 02155, USA

ISBN-13: 978-1-5095-2506-5 (hardback)
ISBN-13: 978-1-5095-2507-2 (paperback)

A catalogue record for this book is available from the British Library.

Library of Congress Cataloging-in-Publication Data
Names: McRobbie, Angela, author.
Title: Feminism and the politics of resilience : Essays on Gender, Media and the End of Welfare / Angela McRobbie.
Description: Medford : Polity, 2020. | Includes bibliographical references and index.
 | Summary: "A captivating analysis of neoliberal culture's hold on womanhood from the leading voice in cultural studies"-- Provided by publisher.
Identifiers: LCCN 2019041734 (print) | LCCN 2019041735 (ebook) | ISBN 9781509525065 (hardback) | ISBN 9781509525072 (paperback) | ISBN 9781509525102 (epub)
Subjects: LCSH: Feminism. | Neoliberalism. | Popular culture--Political aspects.
Classification: LCC HQ1155 .M377 2020 (print) | LCC HQ1155 (ebook) | DDC 305.42--dc23
LC record available at https://lccn.loc.gov/2019041734
LC ebook record available at https://lccn.loc.gov/2019041735

Typeset in 10.5 on 12pt Sabon
by Fakenham Prepress Solutions, Fakenham, Norfolk, NR21 8NL
Printed and bound in Great Britain by TJ Books Limited, Padstow

For further information on Polity, visit our website:
politybooks.com

Contents

Acknowledgements

My thanks are due to the Carl von Ossietzky University, Oldenburg, for the Mercator Fellowship 2017, which allowed me to complete the work for this volume. I presented an early version of Chapter 3 at Oldenburg University *Selbstbildung* Project and wish to thank the colleagues there, especially Thomas Alkemeyer, for their support. I presented Chapter 3 in the Department of Sociology at Vienna University in 2017; thanks are therefore due to Elisabeth Holzleithner, Birgit Sauer and Eva Flicker for inviting me. At Goldsmiths I tried out that chapter at the Centre for Feminist Research 2017; especial thanks to Lisa Blackman for encouraging me to do this. Thanks to Sarah Banet-Weiser for inviting me to present Chapter 2 at the London School of Economics in May 2019.

As ever, I am indebted to Goldsmiths, University of London, and my colleagues in the Department of Media, Communications and Cultural Studies for their enthusiasm and good cheer. I was also able to complete the manuscript thanks to a period of sabbatical leave in 2018. Thanks also to the team at Polity Press for their friendly professionalism and patience.

Chapter 1 appeared in *New Formations*, 81 (2013). I am grateful to the publishers for permission to reprint in this current volume.

Introduction

This short book of just four chapters seeks to develop a feminist account of some contemporary dividing practices associated with our current times of neoliberalism.[1] Each of the essays examines, in different ways, how social polarization is enacted through popular culture[2] and media, and how highly normative ideals of femininity play a role in promoting an increasingly fragmented and splintered society. In a vaguely Butlerian gesture, I understand femininity as a series of historically embedded and institutionally endorsed crafting processes, which take shape and are realized in a wide range of textual and visual practices. These bestow, in ritualistic fashion, modes of recognition on bodies that come to be marked, in their conduct and behaviour as well as appearance, as female. These are also then boundary-marking practices ensuring the perpetuation of heterosexual masculine domination, while also confirming male bodies as in a binary relation with their female counterparts. These crafting processes separate and differentiate the female subject according to class and ethnicity. Femininity, as it is created in the imaginations of the cultural intermediaries of the consumer culture, as well as by various professionals and administrators of the state, is put to use as a mechanism for producing a whole world of distinctions and 'society of inequality' (Bourdieu 1984; Foucault 2006). For example, as shown in Chapter 2, the familiar and quite mundane idea of 'having it all', a staple feminine lifestyle topic of women's magazines and discussion point for high-profile women, which Catherine Rottenberg has subjected to strenuous feminist analysis, becomes an elite call to high-income, mostly young, and almost exclusively liberal-minded white women to separate themselves off, to pull further away, so as to protect their social cachet by finding uniquely middle-class solutions to the predicaments of sustained gender inequities at the upper end of the social spectrum (Rottenberg 2018). We come to know and recognize this privileged class status primarily by visual means and through familiar repertoires which draw attention to slimness, perfected grooming techniques, designer wardrobes, elegant accessories and so on. To be within reach of 'having it all', is already to be significantly and unambivalently upper middle class. Femininity, more so than before, becomes a finely tuned instrument of social calibration; its focus is on the measurement of goals and the meeting of daily objectives.

To an extent, these norms of femininity emanating from consumer culture and from the contemporary polity mark out a continuity with what I described as the field of post-feminism, led by ambitious and competitive 'top girls', for whom feminism as a mass movement was deemed no longer needed, for the reasons of government being seemingly well-disposed to such women as those who might benefit from meritocratic measures, introduced according to the logic of the level playing field (McRobbie 2008; Littler 2017). But this continuity is now interrupted, and in this book I highlight two new elements (there are, of course, many others) that impact on the hegemony of the gender meritocracy and its myth of mobility and opportunity. One is the remarkable and joyful presence of the new feminist campaigning, led primarily by young women, and more typically associated with a left-wing social agenda, and the other is the coming to visibility of women's poverty, revealing what I label the feminine incarceration effect that comes into play for those women who are propelled downwards, and who find themselves locked into a bleak grey landscape from which social mobility becomes virtually impossible. What I have aimed to do across these four essays is to offer an account of the way in which contemporary neoliberal culture operates at an everyday level for women, according to the gradations of class and ethnicity, systematically undoing and ideologically de-legitimizing previous structures of support that had been born in an (albeit short-lived) era where feminists in the 1970s and 1980s had defended non-stigmatizing welfare and where the model of the white, heterosexual family unit was less uncritically embedded; indeed, when feminist academics talked about the 'tyranny of the family' (Barrett and McIntosh 1982). Much of the discussion that follows pivots around questions of work and family life for women in the UK today, as these are refracted through the multi-mediated landscape of entertainment and popular culture. The unifying thread of the contemporary governmentality of young women is the priority of paid work and the significant, but nevertheless secondary, status to be given to family life and intimacy in the guise of what I refer to in Chapter 3 as 'contraceptive employment'. Just to offer an inflection here: for poor, working-class women, including of course those from ethnic minorities, paid employment is a requirement and a prescribed feature of status and identity; for their middle-class counterparts there is the privilege of 'choice', with family, lifestyle and career options interwoven as markers of female success.

The logic of competitive femininity and the loss of a compassionate welfare ethos have led to more openly antagonistic relations visible right across the social fabric, often taking the form of expressions of hatred, cruelty and aggression, as is the case with what has come to be known as the 'poverty-shaming' mechanisms of the tabloid print media and Reality TV. Some early signs of this could be found in television programmes dating back almost twenty years, when upper-middle-class white television presenters such as Trinny Woodhall and Susannah Constantine sneered at the bad taste choices of the working-class women who came forward to be 'made-over' (McRobbie 2008). More recently, feminist media scholars have focused their attention on Reality TV programmes that seek to scandalize more well-heeled viewers through the genre of what de Benedictis et al. label 'Factual Welfare TV', a format that shines a stigmatizing light of media publicity on sectors of the population, typically female, who are poor and reliant on welfare payments (de Benedictis et al. 2017). The success of these programmes, with their huge audiences, has led feminist scholars to interrogate their social meaning, to foreground the injustice of these shaming practices, and to emphasize the highly exploitative formats that portray poor people, mostly poor women, as the victims of their own 'bad choices'. Drawing on this work, my aim here is to propose a stronger connection between critical social policy studies and feminist media and cultural studies, something already outlined in the recent work by Tracey Jensen, who in turn refers back to the path-breaking book by Stuart Hall et al. (Jensen 2018; Hall et al. 1978). The symbolic meaning of social incarceration that unfolds from within the landscapes of Reality TV programmes (such as *Benefits Street*) exposes the fallacy of the mobility ethos inscribed within the idea of meritocracy, while absolutely consolidating and confirming the forms of social polarization that several decades of neoliberal economics and anti-welfare agendas have created. Across Chapters 3 and 4 I reflect on the chasm of social and economic difference that has opened up, and on how previous structures of opportunity have been removed. This incarceration effect could be seen most vividly in yet another Reality TV programme recently broadcast by Channel 4, facetiously titled *Skint: Friends Without Benefits*,[3] which pitched itself, as if in debate with the changes in circumstances to poor communities brought about by the Conservative government's welfare reforms, including the now notorious Universal Credit. Among others, the programme featured a young single mother who was required, as part of her access to benefits, to walk round local shops asking if they had any vacancies. That in every case the answer was a resounding no merely confirmed her abject status, something that encircled all who took part in the programme.

What I am foregrounding here is a kind of cultural analysis that pays attention to how normative femininity articulates a world of small intra-class distinctions, which compel women to endorse and realize ideas of respectability and self-responsibility; and how women who fail to adhere to these principles are subjected to widespread forms of punishment meted out through the instruments of visual media governmentality. The exposure of the bodily failings of profoundly disadvantaged women is accentuated by the new media interfaces, which pitch experts in self-help and make-over culture as mentors, in favour of the more traditional and qualified social workers trained in equal opportunities and in women's rights. Such tactics as these, operating within popular culture, elide entirely the profound material effects of social polarization and incarceral femininity, which have made it well-nigh impossible for poor working-class women, and especially mothers, to improve their situation, on the basis of multiple factors, from the high cost of childcare, to reliance on casual work with unpredictable hours, both of which make it difficult to gain more skills. Again, it is the small details that enforce this state of entrapment; for example new job applications in the lower skill sectors are nowadays pre-filtered by online systems, and recruitment for jobs such as basic office work and administration are outsourced to agencies that oversee the first stage of online applications, so that the chances of being called for an interview, and with this the opportunity perhaps to shine face-to-face, are inevitably curtailed. This acts against women with low levels of qualifications in a wider context, where women in general have acquired higher qualifications, including further and higher education degrees and diplomas. So this sense of failure and of being locked out of opportunities is all the more apparent.

Focusing on the media and popular culture as a favoured public space for debates about liberal feminism in Chapter 1 (which was written in 2012 and first published in 2013), I trace a passage from liberal feminism to neoliberal feminism through the prism of family life and maternity. Where work and employment for women have emerged across the polity as the defining mark of status and womanhood, anxieties that family and parenting must now take second place have led to an intensification, within the world of entertainment, leisure and consumer culture, of attention to family life. So alluring and enjoyable are the new pleasures of the hearth that it becomes incumbent on women to double their efforts after work to become a new kind of 'angel in the house'.[4] This pathway is given a feminist gloss by figures such as Sheryl Sandberg, Chief Operating Officer (COO) of Facebook, who is author of the best-seller titled *Lean In*, and who goes so far as to encourage younger women to look for a pro-feminist type of husband who will willingly do his fair share of household duties and childcare (Sandberg 2012). These ideas play a role in precipitating new seemingly up-to-date models of conservative feminism, of the type endorsed by the former UK Prime Minister, Theresa May, who, at the time of writing Chapter 1, was Home Secretary. This is a resoundingly white middle-class cultural formation of women's citizenship, which, as I show in the chapter, has its historical roots in the late nineteenth century when virtuous white middle-class women were encouraged to envisage their good housekeeping acumen as a kind of professional task and, in so doing, also taking responsibility for the 'future of the race'. I come back in Chapter 4 to the question of colonial power and how that gets to be subsumed into the edifices of the British welfare state. The main argument in Chapter 1 is concerned with this modern-day injunction, realized by means of what I label 'visual media governmentality', to middle-class young women to extend their enthusiasm for their careers, with the proviso that the home too becomes the site of new domestic pleasures, this time with a vaguely feminist gloss, ensuring a shared division of labour in the home. As part of what Wendy Brown refers to as neoliberal rationality, this emphasis on the family as an enterprise that can be worked on for better and more enjoyable 'returns on investment' eliminates all traces of earlier socialist feminist attempts to socialize the family through state investment in nursery provision for all (Brown 2015). No longer is it possible to refer to household duties as drudgery; the task at hand is to find so many new pleasures of the hearth, meanwhile allocating those tasks that entail repetitive and unrewarding labour to low-paid migrant women. In short, I am arguing that privileged middle-class women will aim for leadership jobs in order to crash through the glass ceiling, while also showing themselves to excel in parenting and in creating and maintaining a beautiful home. Their working-class and materially disadvantaged counterparts must prioritize earning a living and taking care of their children as best they can.

In Chapter 2, written some six years later than Chapter 1, there is something of a reversal of neoliberal leadership-feminism, as popular culture proposes what could be envisaged as a move back towards liberal feminism, in the light of the pathologies that contemporary life has exacted on the female subject. The chapter reflects also on two interrelated changes that have interrupted the competitive dynamics of neoliberal rationality as it is directed towards young women. One of these is the anti-capitalist feminism, which has had a remarkable impact, and with this is the specific dilemma that the new era of feminism then poses to the world of consumer culture. Has there been a significant drop in sales of so many beauty products? How does the magazine industry respond to the new demands of seemingly feminist consumers? The other change is the perceived high cost to female 'well-being', which is wrought by the punitive regime of the self-monitoring subject. Sarah Banet-Weiser, extending her previous co-authored work on 'commodity feminism', has undertaken an exhaustive account of how feminism has found its way into the heartland of popular culture, often through the activities of well-known female celebrities who have also welcomed the #MeToo movement (Mukherjee and Banet-Weiser 2012; Banet-Weiser 2018). A whole landscape opens up of female empowerment, which becomes the motif that permits capitalism to make some moves towards welcoming, or even appearing to embrace young women's commitment to feminism.

In Chapter 2, I ponder two related points, asking how far can feminism go in its incursions into the landscape of capitalism's consumer culture before it meets its limits, before it is defined merely as a fad about to pass its sell-by date; before it is once more shunned? If the new feminism mounts an attack on capitalism, what is the response? Banet-Weiser rightly points to the rise of popular misogyny spearheaded by an online culture dominated by young men. I pursue a different tack in this chapter by outlining the emergence of a set of discourses that seek both to supplant and supplement feminism by means of a kind of palliative offering in the form of what I call the 'perfect-imperfect-resilience' or *p-i-r*, which steps forward to offer young women a popular therapeutic strategy that permits some aspects of feminism to be retrieved and drawn upon for support.

With this high visibility of feminism I also draw attention to the argument of Boltanski and Chiapello, who examine the ways in which capitalism has revitalized itself by absorbing elements of the anti-capitalist movements of the late 1960s (social critique or artistic critique) on the basis of their potential for innovation (Boltanski and Chiapello 2005). This leads me to propose that new feminist research projects might look closely, with ethnographic detail, at the cultural producers, including the gatekeeper, editors and other decision-makers; in particular those people who are charged with this task of translation.

The second issue I reflect on connects with the perceived harms to women of competition and endless self-assessment. Here I draw attention to the politics of resilience, which in turn entails a scaling down of the principles of neoliberal 'leadership-feminism' in favour of a more ordinary and less exceptional set of expectations. Liberal feminism proves itself to be more accommodating to the management of self for the modern-day middle-class gender regime. With such an emphasis on the widespread mental ill health of the female subject I also query the absence of a feminist psycho-analytical vocabulary, which would interrogate the basis of this female complaint and the prevalence of self-beratement. The writing of Adam Phillips and also Judith Butler permits a pathway away from the tyranny of the sovereign self in favour of a more relational and dependent idea of the subject who asks, from the start: 'Who are you?'

Chapter 2 brings together, then, three specific themes: the displacement function played by the *p-i-r*; the profit from feminism; and the need for an ethics of care and of vulner-ability by means of a psychoanalytical feminism, which de-centres the sovereign self, opening up an unstable female subjectivity as livable in her relation to others. Overall, the chapter reveals some of the tensions that emerge in relation to the driving force of a neoliberal leadership-feminism that has gripped hold of so many popular discourses and textual artefacts directed at women.

In Chapter 3, the focus of attention is on what is required for a feminist cultural studies perspective on the social polarization effect born out of more than three decades of neoliberalism in the UK. This entails a critique of the work of prominent Marxists David Harvey and Wolfgang Streeck for their inattention to sociologically important changes to the gender regime. The writing of Stuart Hall provides a stronger steer for investigating the way in which political economy is translated at ground level to transform the vocabularies that prevail in the workplace, the home and the local neighbourhood. It is everyday language, in particular that deployed by the tabloid press, which implants a new terminology of welfare and which provides a groundswell for public approval to cuts to benefit payments on the grounds of claimants being typecast as feckless, cheating and lazy. Women, especially single mothers, are poverty-shamed, and this drives a further wedge not just between these working-class women and their middle-class counter-parts but also at an intra-class level. This suggests that the anti-welfare agenda comprises a moving horizon to target the majority of the low paid who are also current recipients of in-work benefits. There is a war of attrition reminding us of how key to neoliberal rationality is the attack on social democracy as the guarantor (within limits) of welfare. (In fact, social democrats have been at the forefront of the drive to reduce welfare since the mid 1990s, but it has proved even more integral to the neoliberal project to get rid of any lingering traces.) There is substantial pressure on women not just to be employed, but also to prioritize working life and to abide by the rules of 'contraceptive employment'. If there is a shaming effect on single mothers as they come to embody all the failings of welfare dependency, the logic is to avoid this status except under exceptional circumstances, such as an abusive relationship. The stigmatizing stereo-types and the demeaning images are also boundary-marking activities, which enact a vernacular of social polarization on a day-to-day basis.

In Chapter 4, I more fully interrogate the landscape of poverty-shaming, looking specifically at Reality TV, where I also pay attention to racializing logics, which append whiteness at that point at which working-class women lose the privilege of being deemed without race on the basis of their downward mobility. The figure I consider, who starred in the series *Benefits Street*, was named White Dee to differ-entiate her from her friend and neighbour, who was black

(Dee Samora). The programme demonstrates so many of the microscopic tensions and contradictions of popular culture to which I referred in note 2 of this introduction. Even as she is shamed, White Dee embodies proud, unbowed working-class femininity. She asserts herself as someone with moral capacity supporting her neighbours by escorting them to hospital or helping them with benefit problems. She also challenges the stereotypes of the welfare scrounger heaped upon herself and her neighbours by the tabloid press and by wider audiences providing online comments. Following through on the politics of race within debates on welfare, I conclude the chapter by referencing the work of so many black scholars who have drawn attention to the positioning of black people as outside welfare in its entirety and seen as undeserving subjects, whose labour is nevertheless required in order for the welfare apparatus to operate for the benefit of white British society. This racial logic of the British welfare state forces a rewriting of any even vaguely rosy account of the achievements of social democracy in this respect, forcing also reconsideration of the times of the so-called 'affluent worker' (Shilliam 2018; Virdee 2019).

I end this book with some brief ruminations on social polarization and the intensification of poverty, which are all but disguised by the emphasis, now so firmly established in the popular imagination, on welfare cheats and benefit 'scroungers'. Arguably women who do rely on benefits, in or out of work, now find themselves more emphatically symbolically incarcerated than was the case in the past. The precarious lives they are forced to lead must be done so without the trained advisers and support workers who might have been able to utilize a non-stigmatizing vocabulary, which was in place from the mid 1970s, before being replaced by the new system of public management some twenty years later. Thus, we see neoliberalism proceed by multiple processes of substitution and displacement. Kinder words and more equal encounters are edged out of social interactions with vulnerable sectors of the population. Spaces,[5] images and words are made to comply with the requirements of the boundary-marking practices that enforce stricter social polarization, giving rise to new forms of daily antagonism and aggression. To undo this whole terrain of everyday life and institutional culture, feminist scholars and activists would need to imagine a new and quite different social field predicated on reparative and restorative welfare and a municipal commons comprising public spaces that would counter the incarceration effect. Alongside this we might also envisage forms of media and popular culture that would refute the genres which currently continue to degrade those who have suffered from the intensification of poverty.

1
Feminism, the Family and the New Multi-Mediated Maternalism

The Maternal–Feminine

In this first chapter[1] I trace a line of development from liberal to neoliberal feminism, which is, I claim, being at least partly realized and embodied through the ubiquitous figure of the middle-class, professional wife and mother. Following on from a comment by Stuart Hall on the centrality of the 'middle class' to the neoliberal project, I overlay this with the additional categories of gender and maternity (Hall 2011). This emergent image of motherhood not only displaces, but also begins to dismantle, a longstanding political relationship, which in the UK has linked post-war social democracy with maternity, while simultaneously providing the political right with a new, more contemporary script that allows it to take the lead in the current debate on family life. The analysis I offer is restricted, more or less, to contemporary Britain, with several references to US popular culture and to US liberal feminism, for the reason that these have provided so much of a steer for the way in which the neoliberal agenda in the UK has addressed motherhood and domestic life. This agenda is quite different from the now out-of-date conservative mantra of 'family values'. The right-wing newspaper the *Daily Mail* in its 'Femail' section has been particularly forceful in its championing of a style of affluent, feminine maternity. This idea of active (en route to the gym), sexually confident motherhood marks an extension of its pre-maternal equivalent, the ambitious and aspirational young working woman or 'top girl' (McRobbie 2008). It is also consistently pitched against an image of the abject, slovenly and benefits-dependent single mother, the UK equivalent of the US 'welfare Mom'. (The political role of this imaginary of welfare maternity is explored in more detail in Chapters 3 and 4 of this volume.) Only in academic feminism do we find a more critical and empathetic response to the difficulties faced by out-of-work single mothers.[2]

While feminism has for many decades been a political formation with historic connection closer to the left than the right, this alignment is now undergoing change, with substantial gains for the right should it manage to develop further what is at the moment merely a kind of feminist flourish. Within and alongside the UK Coalition government we could see a fledgling feminist strand, led mostly by an urban, upper-middle-class stratum of women, including former Cabinet Minister Louise Mensch, Home Secretary Theresa May, Liberal Democrat MP Jo Swinson, as well as a number of influential young spokeswomen from right-wing think tanks such as Policy Reform. This tacit endorsement of feminism is informed by 1970s US liberal feminism, with an emphasis on equal rights, condemnation of domestic and sexual violence, and action against genital mutilation. It is drawn into the field of popular Tory neoliberal hegemony particularly through the idea of 'welfare reform', and in this realm it takes the form of an unapologetically middle-class white feminism, shorn of all obligations to less privileged women or to those who are not 'strivers' (a favoured term within welfare reform discourse).

In what is, I hope, a continuation of feminist discussions on the rise of neoliberalism led by Wendy Brown's work on the demise of liberal democracy, and followed through by my own writing on young women as subjects of the meritocracy under New Labour, and by Nancy Fraser in her provocative argument that there has been 'feminist complicity', I aim to show how a new momentum for the political right is accomplished by means of a careful claiming of heterosexual maternal womanhood (Brown 2005; McRobbie 2008; Fraser

2009). What has emerged is a perhaps unexpected rehabilitation of feminism as a broad constellation of progressive socio-political interests converging around the category of woman that can be usefully deployed by those modernizing forces of the right, centre and also centre left, where previously such an association would have been shunned. The very words 'conservative feminism' are now commonplace, part of the everyday vocabulary of Louise Mensch in her newspaper articles, blogs and television appearances and a lively talking point across contemporary political culture in the UK. Feminism is no longer despised but is given new life through an articulation with a specific range of values pertaining to the project of contemporary neoliberalism. This connection is confirmed towards the end of the bestselling book *Lean In: Women, Work and the Will to Lead* by the Chief Operating Officer (COO) of Facebook, Sheryl Sandberg, where the author unashamedly declares herself a feminist (Sandberg 2012). I will return to Sandberg's book and its significance in the final section of this chapter, but for the moment I want to highlight this take-up of feminism as an aspect of the ambitious reach of neoliberalism – a breadth of influence that means that its principles have become not just a new kind of common-sense, but also an active force-field of political values, at a time when the political left has been crushed or at least subdued.[3] Others would remark that parties of both the left and (centre) left have in any case already conceded to the neoliberal agenda, such that there is not a great deal of difference in the UK between the modernizing agenda of Labour and the austerity-driven policies of the Coalition government. In each case there has been a commitment to privatization of the public sector, the denigration of welfare regimes as producing unaffordable dependencies, an emphasis on self-responsibility and entrepreneurialism, and constant advocacy of stable (if also now flexible and gay) forms of family life.

As a starting point, then, I would say that there is something of a feminist endorsement detectable in the political air. The animosity and repudiation, which were features of the Blair government and the popular culture and media of the time, have receded. Support for 'hard-working families', a phrase first coined by Gordon Brown during his time as Chancellor of the Exchequer, was retained by both leaders of the Tory Party and the Liberal Democrats, but this now incorporates a more engaged and sympathetic dialogue with mothers (stay-at-home and working), with some indication that this is a 'feminist issue' for today.[4] This advocacy of women seems like more than just a pragmatic move to secure the female vote, and more than a knee-jerk response to the vocal presence of online campaigners and new female constituencies. Instead it is arguably part of a process of inventing a repertoire of woman-centred positions that will confirm and enhance the core values of the neoliberal project. A great deal of this ideological work takes place outside, but in close proximity to, the field of formal politics, in culture and in particular within the various forms of feminine mass media:[5] including BBC Radio 4's *Woman's Hour*; the 'Femail' section of the *Daily Mail* mentioned above; the 'women's pages' (or 'lifestyle' sections) of all the national quality daily newspapers such as the *Guardian*, the *Independent*, *The Times* and the *Daily Telegraph*; some key daytime television programmes such as *Loose Women*; and, of course, the range of women's magazines from the fashion-oriented *Grazia* to *Red* and *Elle* and the traditional *Woman's Own*. Where in the early 2000s an invitation to female empowerment seemed to require a ritualistic denunciation of feminism as old-fashioned and no longer needed (with the exception of the left-leaning *Guardian* newspaper and BBC Radio 4's *Woman's Hour*), the current media culture now feels able to make a claim, of sorts, to a feminism, of sorts.

The observations I offer in the pages that follow suggest the value of a feminism (with roots in the US liberal feminist tradition) for the neoliberal regime, offering a distinctively gendered dimension to the mantra of individualism, the market and competition as well as updating the now old-fashioned 'family values' vocabularies associated with social conservatism. These are old-fashioned for a number of reasons. For a start, female labour power is far too important to the post-industrial economy for anyone to be an advocate of long-term stay-at-home wives and mothers. Moreover, spurred on by the rise of feminism from the mid 1970s onwards, women expressed a strong desire to work. (LGBTQ and BAME women, along with their working-class white counterparts, have always been in paid labour.) The new conservative feminists see that with the high rate of divorce, having a career not only provides women with an income and independence, it also reduces the cost of welfare to government. It thus makes sense for government to champion women who will enter the labour market and stay in it. In this context the new 'corporate' feminism supports and extends the dominance of contemporary neoliberalism. If it runs into some difficulties when confronted, for example, by religious lobbies and individual politicians of both sexes opposed to abortion (or similar issues), these are surmountable obstacles. Choice, empowerment and a commitment to 'planned parenthood' are uppermost.

Imperative to this new neoliberal feminism is its stand and status with regard to its imagined other, the Muslim woman assumed to be oppressed and subjected to various forms of domination and control. Various feminist scholars writing in the context of the post 9/11 world have referred to this as the instrumentalization of feminism, and Jasbir Puar has reflected on the strategic value of homonationalism, and the instrumentalization of gay and lesbian rights, as a means by which Western governments, particularly in the US, can assert a kind of global progressive superiority (Puar 2012). What I am interested to chart here is the way in which, working through a number of powerful media channels, political parties and forces of the mainstream right – primarily, in my account, the British Conservatives, but also parties in Europe such as the German Christian Democrats – are able to revitalize and modernize the conservative agenda by adopting a weak version of feminism, which in turn permits a new kind of more attentive address to women.[6]

Revolutionary Road?

In what follows I first introduce the analysis of family values and neoliberal feminism by briefly considering the 2009 film *Revolutionary Road* (dir. Sam Mendes). I then look back at some strands of (second-wave) socialist–feminist writing on the family from the late 1970s. This is followed by a section on the Foucault tradition, especially the late 1970s biopolitics lectures and the concept of human capital. And then, as a tool for understanding the new address to mothers as active sexual subjects (expressed through body culture) as well as subjects who are proactive in the economic sense (in the workforce), I propose 'visual media governmentality' as a regulatory space for the formulation and working through of many of these ideas. It is here that the bench-marks and boundaries of female success are established, and it is here that new norms of failure symbolized in the abject body of the 'single mother' and in the bodies of her untidy children or 'brood' are to be found. In this visual field, vulnerability and dependency are graphically equated with personal carelessness, with being overweight and badly dressed, and these in turn become 'performance indicators' signalling inadequate life planning and what Wendy Brown calls 'mismanaged lives' (Brown 2005).

Why *Revolutionary Road*? This is a film positioned somewhere between the popular middlebrow, quasi-independent films associated with the Working Title productions of Richard Curtis, films often appealing primarily to women, and a more art-house genre. This generic slot promises a largely female, middle-class, possibly university-educated audience. Such are the complex economies of film production and distribution today that at the time of the cinematic release there are multiple strands of accompanying publicity and snippets of information widely disseminated across a range of media forms, with the result that films become remarkably open-ended cultural objects. *Revolutionary Road* reunited two of Hollywood's most famous actors already known for their previous performance in *Titanic*, and in this sense the stars Kate Winslet and Leonardo DiCaprio bring to the film a whole set of both sexual and romantic expec-tations. The director Sam Mendes was at the time married to Kate Winslet and the film itself is about marital discord. Mendes is known for directing *American Beauty*, and he is regarded as someone with a liberal sensibility.

Both *American Beauty* and *Revolutionary Road* have small casts, like stage-plays, and they are prepared to tackle difficult emotional situations, underscored by a recognition of the place for, and impact of, sexual politics. If *American*

Beauty told a story of post-feminist heterosexual family life, *Revolutionary Road* turns the director's gaze back in time to pre-(liberal-)feminist USA. Based on a highly regarded novel published in 1962 by US writer Richard Yates, *Revolutionary Road* offers the opportunity to reflect on a move from the founding moments of white, middle-class US liberal feminism to its contemporary transformation into neoliberal feminism. It is a film that has as its subtext a range of feminist issues, serving as a reminder of the gains made in the moment coming directly after the period in which the film is set. It is not so much that it anticipates feminism as that it shows why, when it finally exploded, US liberal feminism took the shape that it did. It is therefore an immanent narrative fuelled by an unspeakable desire for something, which could only be a sexual politics to come. The timing of its production, the themes that the director does not quite bring to the surface, but leaves to the audience to infer, as well as a press comment by Kate Winslet that she read *The Feminine Mystique* in preparation for the role of April, all suggest that the producers of this multi-million-dollar film were persuaded that feminist questions could translate into box-office success.[7] Set in the mid 1950s, the film, however, offers no evoking of nostalgia. Winslet's wardrobe is carefully chosen both to constrain her within that pre-feminist moment of conservative femininity and also to suggest that she is pushing the boundaries of convention. She is more urban and elegant than her neighbours, and her clothes encapsulate her yearning to be somewhere else. This is a film located in that US post-war suburban moment as a pre-feminist stage before the storm bursts, and it depicts a litany of feminist concerns explored through the character of April, but without naming them as such.

   The couple April and Frank find themselves locked into a lifestyle that bears all the marks of white post-war American affluence, and all the rigidities of gender and sexuality that underpinned the new nuclear family of the period. April's hopes for a career in acting are dashed after a humiliation in a local amateur dramatics performance. She also sees that her husband is unfulfilled in his desk job, and so she proposes a move to Paris. April's enthusiasm is first curbed by the hard work she has to do to win her husband over to this plan, and then extinguished when two events follow each other in quick succession: first she gets pregnant with a third child and wants an abortion, which shocks Frank; and then he in turn gets an unexpected promotion at work, while at the same time compensating for suburban boredom by enjoying the frisson of adultery with a girl from the office pool. As the relationship crumbles, April flirts with one of the neighbours when they find themselves alone together after a couples' night out, and she has sex with him in the car, rejecting him a few days later. She then infuriates her husband by getting hold of an obstetric vacuum to carry out an abortion and, when he confesses to having had an affair, she merely asks him angrily why he bothered to tell her. Paris is no longer an option and in despair April aborts herself, rupturing her womb and haemorrhaging to death. The film closes with shots of the bereaved father Frank, now relocated to New York City, watching his kids play in the park, as the realtor neighbours back in the suburbs comment on how the couple never really fitted in.

These are the years before easily available birth control, never mind safe abortions, when ambitious women, with the onset of motherhood, were rarely able to fulfil themselves with a career. The film shows the claustrophobia of family life and motherhood as triggers for what was to come: the women's movement (or revolution) of the mid 1960s. It contains a catalogue of soon-to-be feminist issues. The question of female sexual pleasure is explored when April enjoys seducing her neighbour, but the sex act itself only lasts a few seconds. Once it is done it is over. Nor does April display any significant affection for her children; maternity is simply something that happened to her unbidden. Overall the film implicitly makes the strongest argument in favour of divorce. The narrative suggests that female mental health and well-being can depend on being able to exit a marriage, and gain independence – a life of one's own.

It is the timing of the film that was significant in the context of its reception in the UK and US. The film fed into anxieties about the breakdown of marriage and the de-stabilizing of family life. It introduced feminist issues for a middle-class audience segment unused to the intrusion of angry sexual politics within the landscape of contemporary cinema. Maybe it introduced gender discord and sexual politics within the ranks of the political right, if the review by Charles Moore in the *Daily Telegraph* is anything to go by.[8] In any case, my argument here is that the film marks a point of contestation in a popular film culture, which for the previous decade had celebrated weddings, and which has humorously portrayed young women's fears of missing out on marriage and children, and of 'always being the bridesmaid and never the bride'.[9] *Revolutionary Road*, with its Hollywood stars, demonstrates its liberal credentials by contesting the sanctity of marriage. The film serves as a reminder of the contribution of liberal feminism to contemporary Western women's freedoms. Through the narrative of April, the film anticipates the 'revolutionary' change that was just around the corner. The film reminds its viewers of the idea of progress: there can be no return to a time when married women were trapped in the home with only the chores of babies and housework to punctuate the day. The narrative bolsters a linear model of progress along with the idea of personal or individual liberation. There is a profoundly white liberal feminist 'structure of feeling' running through *Revolutionary Road*. Kate Winslet in and out of character offers a powerful point of identification for young, middle-class women today. She is beautiful and successful, and she exudes an aura of being a passionate and independent woman. As the *Daily Mail* sourly noted, following the announcement of her pregnancy, she would soon be the mother of three children, all of whom have different fathers, a so-called '3 x 3'. (I return to this colloquial shaming and disparaging of the single mother in Chapters 3 and 4 of this volume.)

The Nursery as Socialist Ideal

I have argued so far that contemporary neoliberalism, in its bid to embed itself more deeply as a new kind of common-sense, enters into a symbiotic relationship with liberal feminism, extending its remit to endorse the working, married, almost exclusively white, heterosexual mother. I have also pointed to the significant role allocated to the professional middle-class mother in this hegemony-building exercise. But who exactly is she? We could point to the modes of visibility and publicity management that surrounded leading politicians' wives, such as Samantha Cameron and Miriam Clegg. We could also include COO of Facebook Sheryl Sandberg in this list of 'female highflyers' (as the press describes them); mothers who, whether temporarily on sabbatical from their careers, or else 'juggling' and combining work with motherhood, nevertheless embark on the latter with professional attention to duty, responsibility and all the skills required to ensure a stable upbringing for children. In effect, they are called upon to be 'exemplary' mothers within a political culture intent on reversing family breakdown, and on encouraging better and more effective parenthood. But it is the website www.mumsnet.co.uk that most precisely embodies this new role of professional middle-class maternity, and which now has achieved the status of a mother's lobby. This model of maternal citizenship is counter-posed in the popular press and tabloids, as I have already noted above, by an abject maternal figure, typically a single mother with several children fathered by different men, reliant on benefits, living in a council house, and with an appearance that suggests lack of attention to body image, all of which within today's moral universe implies fecklessness, promiscuity and inade-quate parenting. the *Daily Mail* once again takes the lead in exposing these examples of bad mothers, many of whom are shown either to be cheating the welfare system, bringing up delinquent children, never to have had a job or else to have failed to provide their children with reliable father figures. In July 2013, the *Daily Mail* commissioned respected British Asian writer and broadcaster Yasmin Alibhai-Brown to spend a day in a neighbourhood that the journalist describes disparagingly as a 'man desert', on the basis of the seemingly high number of single mothers, many of whom in this case were black.[10] More often, articles like this rely on photo-graphs of unruly looking children alongside a tired and untidy-looking mother, where, as Beverley Skeggs would argue, such an appearance has become synonymous with unrespectable and morally deficient working-class femininity (Skeggs 1997).

This whole vista of information, publicity and news exists within a frame where social and political affairs merge, often to be overtaken by the world of entertainment and celebrity culture. In effect, some of the most pressing social issues of our times, such as 'welfare reform', are wrapped up in a confection of what used to be known as 'tit-bits', gossip, in a contemporary version of what Richard Hoggart referred to as the traditional 'Peg's Paper' style of reading material designed for a large popular female readership and audience (Hoggart 1957). An allusion to Hoggart is particularly appropriate because what is also entirely missing from this new world of either exemplary or shameful maternity is the figure of the strong, working-class mother, the kind of stalwart of the community that Hoggart, and before him D. H. Lawrence, described so vividly. Not particularly concerned about her appearance, often tired, sometimes holding down several poorly paid jobs at once, making sure her children were well fed and got the best opportunities, this figure has almost gone from the popular imagination. She lingers on only as the occasional character in TV soap operas such as *Coronation Street*, and when she does make an appearance in other television genres it is as the hard-pressed Mum in need of a make-over, whose children or husband will connive with the television presenters to offer her the chance for some radical transformation that will bring her up to the standard of glamorous visual appearance now required to count as a woman today. In other words, she is subjected to the normalizing horizon of beauty culture that brings working-class women somehow within reach of middle-class aspiration, sexual attractiveness and hence social acceptability (McRobbie 2008). The disappearance of the working-class mother as someone with any public voice or visibility – never mind the respect and dignity such a figure was once accorded in left-wing thought as well as in literature, drama and cinema – is instructive in this shifting political universe where social democracy is in decline, welfare is widely derided as wasteful and there are fewer voices in politics, media or in public policy fields willing to defend them in principle.

   To unpack further the starkness of this transformation and the withdrawal of compassion and support to women who as mothers find themselves trapped in welfare dependency, we need to reflect on the historical relationship that existed between both radical and social democratic politics and feminism, especially with regard to maternity, for the reason that it is this set of intersecting political forces that has been trounced and overshadowed by the ascendancy of the new right, the centre right and the centre left, inaugurated by the Clinton government in the US (with its singling out of the racializing trope of 'welfare queens' as the focus of attention in the bid to make workfare the only option) and consolidated as the Third Way during the Blair years. Indeed, we cannot underestimate the zeal with which the Blair government set about dismantling old Labour allegiances. This also involved a scornful repudiation of feminism and a discrediting of the value and place of labour history.

Of course, it is not as though feminism had ever existed in comfortable harmony with the Labour Party. The schisms between Labour and the extra-parliamentary left, including the socialist-feminists from the 1970s through to the 1990s, are well documented. Most of the best-known writing on feminism and the family emerged from Marxist–feminist scholarship, including the work of Elizabeth Wilson (1975), Michèle Barrett and Mary McIntosh (1982), and also the historical writing of Denise Riley (1986). None of these writers was directly connected to the Labour Party and many were fiercely critical of the reformist tendencies of social democracy. Yet this divide was not entirely impermeable and, by the mid 1980s, several Marxist groups had dissolved and entered the Labour Party, while the British Communist Party, including the well-known feminist journalist Bea Campbell, shared many political platforms and indeed journals with prominent figures inside Labour, especially as it moved to embrace a more mainstream Euro-Communism. If the heroic years of the Labour Party occurred during the post-war period, then it is also the case that through these decades there were many activists and campaigners inside and alongside the party who were committed to improving living standards for families, especially those who found themselves in financial hardship. It was women inside Labour who also lobbied to ensure that child benefits could be paid directly to the mother, and who fought hard to establish pre-school provision, especially in low-income neighbourhoods. The Child Poverty Action Group was influential for many years and for a period was headed by Ruth Lister, a highly regarded feminist scholar as well as campaigner, who for decades has been involved in (among other things) defending poor, single mothers against attempts by government to push them into work, despite the difficulties in securing good quality full-time nursery provision.[11]

The Blair period of modernization set in place a momentum that marginalized, discredited or cast as old-fashioned this kind of feminist policy work, with the result that, apart from the Women's Budget Group and the 'gender mainstreaming' platform, women's voices were muted and more or less ignored.[12] This demise is arguably a key factor in the rise of the new binaries of good and bad motherhood that now litter the popular press and media. Despite the emergence of new feminist online campaigners and activists from 2008 onwards, little of their attention has been paid to defending poor women against cuts to welfare. Nor have these online organizations tackled the disapproval and disapprobation of poor, single mothers, or challenged the glamorization of motherhood found across the popular media, which concentrates only on the super-wealthy and celebrities who have access to as many nannies as they need. Feminist public policy research in journals such as *Critical Social Policy* does span this range of topics, interrogating for example the wider impact of this negative stereotyping of single mothers, and there have also been a number of articles in *MAMSIE* challenging the new moral landscape of motherhood.[13] What is missing is a wider contextualization of the demonization of the disadvantaged within a socio-cultural framework, which charts not just the decline of social democracy, but also the fact that this passing away is strangely unmarked and hence unmourned.

If we do pay attention to what was a defining feature of the UK welfare state in the early years, that is, the important place occupied by women and children as rightful subjects of entitlements and benefits, we can nevertheless be reminded of how the social security system was predicated on a white male breadwinner model, which by the late 1970s was being challenged by socialist feminists, who argued for women's full participation in the labour force as a means of gaining and retaining economic independence. With this the question of childcare provision suddenly comes to the forefront. Three key texts from this period reflect exactly the terrain of debate: Elizabeth Wilson's *Women and the Welfare State* (1975); Michèle Barrett and Mary McIntosh's *The Anti-Social Family* (1982); and Denise Riley's *War in the Nursery* (1986).

Riley's rich historical account charted the angry debates that raged within the ranks of the medical experts, psycho-analysts and other professionals about the role of nursery care, and this in turn brought to the attention of feminists the idea of 'socialized childcare', something also associated with Communist states. This idea found great favour within different strands of feminism in the UK, for various reasons: first, that only full-time nursery care freed women to enter employment, gain economic independence, and pursue uninterrupted careers, thus fulfilling their potential as equal to men in work and professional life; second, that the nursery environment was beneficial for children, allowing them to gain social skills and escape the over-heated and exclusive emotional connection with the mother; and third, that exclusive motherhood was in any case a trap for women, an exhausting, unrewarding role, one of servitude without pay. Well-organized nursery provision was a socialist idea, almost from the start. Nursery provision was a key feature both of feminist discourse and of wider public policy discussion for more than forty years. Labour governments had seen nursery care as a way of improving the health and well-being of children from poor families, while also allowing women to work and hence contribute to family incomes. While feminist theorists, especially Elizabeth Wilson, pointed to the policing role of welfare as it intruded into the lives of working-class families, there was nevertheless a consistent support within feminism for state-provided nursery care alongside paid maternity leave, and other related provisions.

The Anti-Social Family is also instructive to look back at, not just because it tackles the oppressive aspects of domesticity and the 'tyranny of maternity' but also because it acknowledges the exclusion of lesbian women, who at the time had few possibilities for maternity and who also suffered the stigma of childlessness. In many ways this book articulates the divide between the perceived privi-leges of heterosexual feminism and its championing of motherhood as a priority within feminism, and the pre-queer dynamics of marginalization from normative family life. At the same time, Michèle Barrett and Mary McIntosh fully recognize the apparently endless popularity of the family in everyday life and the unlikelihood of its demise. In the light of this seemingly consensual enjoyment of the domestic sphere, feminists arguably withdrew from extreme anti- or alternative-family positions and instead became involved in campaigns that supported mothers through a range of measures, notably maternity leave, flexible working hours, as well as access to affordable childcare.[14] I stress this historical trajectory not as an uninterrupted pathway but rather to emphasize the troubled but nevertheless anchored connection between feminism and the pro-active policies associated with social democratic governments, which supported women's movement into work from the early 1970s onwards and, concomitant with this, recognized pre-school childcare as being socially as well as financially beneficial.

What has happened from early 2000 with regard to this configuration of once powerful forces is instructive. The feminist emphasis on the 'tyrannny of maternity' (as Barrett and McIntosh put it) has become utterly unspeakable, as has the portrayal of housework and childcare as drudgery. It would be interesting to speculate as to why there is at present, despite various other feminist actions, no organization or campaign that addresses the oppressive, repetitive, exhausting nature of daily housework and childcare and the extent to which women are still disproportionately responsible for these daily responsibilities. Perhaps this can be attributed to the legacy of a post-feminist culture that emphasizes responsibility and choice. As various sociologists have argued, structural issues are transformed into personal matters for which private solutions must be found.[15] The ideological force of choice has a de-socializing and de-politicizing function. But, more emphatically, the idea of affordable socialized childcare (i.e. mass nursery care) as a universal provision is also unthinkable, as a result of its socialist, communist and welfare-ist heritage, and thus its cost to the state. In this context, full-time nursery provision for babies and toddlers has been conveniently discredited as harmful to children.[16] And yet this model provided the single most effective route out of poverty for disadvantaged and single-parent households. For mothers to participate fully in the labour market there has to be an extensive and well-run programme of childcare and after-school care. Without this, working mothers will always have mixed feelings about prioritizing wage labour.

The nexus of social democratic and feminist politics that was for many years a defining feature of Labour policies in the UK, shaping the nature of thinking on families, welfare and maternity, found itself at least by-passed, if not thrown out, by the forces of modernization associated with the Blair period. Banal phrases like the 'work–life balance' came to replace more sustained debate about how motherhood and work could realistically be combined, without women jeopardizing their opportunities in the workplace. Implicitly, there was a return to gender traditionalism, as women were urged to compromise in the workplace so as to maintain a dual role, this representing a step back from all feminist arguments for gender equality and the equal sharing of domestic roles. Few women at the time were prepared to argue loudly for men to compromise on their careers or prospects for promotion in favour of sharing all household responsibilities, as to say such a thing would merely confirm a feminist anti-men stance, which during the Blair years was quite unacceptable within the landscape of Westminster politics.[17]

To sum up, to understand the new family values of the present moment it is necessary to look back to the New Labour period and to the way in which previous historical affiliations between social democracy and feminism, which aimed to support women as mothers, were dismantled and discredited. This opened the way for the present-day demonization of welfare as though to suggest that relying on support or subsidy is somehow shameful. Thus families need to take responsibility for their own affairs and not look to the state for 'hand-outs'. At the same time there is a widely disseminated discourse that celebrates choice and the privatization of childcare through the use of nannies. The granting of marital and parental rights to lesbian and gay couples, while important and just, has further consolidated in popular culture and the media a kind of hermetic ideal of family life that undercuts the older social democratic systems of provision for families including youth clubs, girls' groups, and a wide array of leisure facilities such as municipal swimming pools, tennis courts, libraries and community centres – all of which exist outside the domestic space. These at the same time provided many occasions for undertaking urban anti-sexist and anti-racist work, and for breaking down class divisions among children.

Good Housekeeping: The Biopolitics of the Family

Feminist historians, such as Anna Davin, Catherine Hall and Leonore Davidoff have investigated the entanglements of class, race and sexuality, which have accompanied the politics of maternity and family life over a period of more than two hundred years (Davin 1978; Davidoff and Hall 2002). This influential work has pinpointed, among other things, the exemplary status accorded to the middle-class family, especially in the Victorian period, and the maternal citizenship role allocated to the virtuous mother who was also the 'Angel in the House'. To the feminist sociologist today, the writing of Foucault and scholars influenced by him supplements this feminist history, allowing for an extrapolation from history, so that certain reiterated processes can be gleaned as central to the 'birth of the social' and to contemporary modes of managing the family. The disciplining of unruly, excessively fertile, female, working-class and colonial bodies entailed, for example, an accumulation and organization of knowledge, as well as the training of experts to administer various techniques designed to rein in and control women's sexual activity. As we know from Foucault, huge apparatuses of the state came into being to form a government of populations with the nuclear family unit replacing the proliferation of wild and deviant sexualities, all of which were to be censored, as the 'parental bedroom' took precedence as the sanctified space for the satisfaction of desires (Foucault 1987). Donzelot, writing about nineteenth-century France, followed this line of argument, showing how the new administrative class struggled with the unruly habits of working-class women who on the one hand too easily abandoned their own babies into the care of the state, while at the same time they provided defective or inadequate care to their middle-class charges, whom they were paid both to wet nurse and to look after through childhood (Donzelot 1979). The fear of inculcation of bad habits to the future dominant class led to action being taken to give new status and responsibility to the white middle-class mother herself, in effect making her role official, and encouraging a close relationship with the medical profession. She was from now on to be in charge of the 'future of the race'.[18]

Neither Foucault nor Donzelot draws attention to the imperialist mission embedded in these processes, nor to the role accorded to white women in securing processes of colonial dominance. Nor either do they mention the historical genre of the women's magazine as the point of dissemination for this (colonialist) educative and instructive activity. It has been the task of feminist scholars to undertake this, by looking at the various technologies of the 'advice column' or the 'problem page' as instrumental in the training of white middle-class young women. Practices of cleanliness, hygiene and the whole business of good housekeeping were the focus of attention in these pages, and this was extended, according to the precise class location of readers, to include fashion, beauty and rituals around the social calendar and courtship. Not only has this genre provided the format for modern-day women's magazines and television programmes, it has also demonstrated the centrality of looking as well as reading for this realm of informal domestic and personal pedagogy. The question remains, however, as to how exactly these forms functioned as 'dividing practices', demarcating and policing the boundaries of class and ethnicity, censoring inappropriate knowledges and removing unsuitable material from the gaze of the white middle-class readership. Here we could point to the editor emerging as an important figure within the ranks of the professional-managerial class, the person who both exemplifies and oversees this field of feminine taste and decorum. As various historians pointed out, the intoxicating pleasures of fashion, fabric and home-making found inside these pages came to the attention of the lower classes and subsequently had a powerful impact in diverting working-class girls and women's desires away from their status in life, in the direction of emulating middle-class lifestyles (Bowlby 1985; Felski 1995; Walkowitz 1985). This in turn produced tensions and anxieties from many different directions. In many respects they were doing what was being requested of them pedagogically: mimicking the manners and good habits of their superiors, though only within certain prescribed limits. There were immediately fears that they would get ideas above their station in life and that an interest in finery would distract them from the labour discipline of the factory floor. And, as Caroline Steedman showed in her remarkable book, *Landscape for a Good Woman*, these feminine pleasures also created aspiration to social betterment and a desire to escape a working-class life (Steedman 1986).

Foucault's Biopolitics Lectures delivered in the mid 1970s also focus on good housekeeping as part of the neoliberal programme developed through the writing of the Ordoliberals in Germany in the early 1930s. Roepke for example saw the family as to be managed along the lines of a small business or enterprise, and Foucault describes the human capital model of the child in the family as an 'abilities machine'. This notion of enterprise is, argues Foucault, central to the programme of neoliberalization, and if we move away from these historical examples to the present day it is possible to see that by casting the family as a small business a new rationale for 'gender retraditionalization' emerges, as Lisa Adkins has persuasively shown (Adkins 1999). The family becomes a partnership of equals, even if this means a stay-at-home Mum and full-time working father. In contemporary parlance such a traditional arrangement reflects a modern team-like decision, one which could be easily reversed.

Once again, the emphasis Foucault places on human capital permits an account of how new norms of middle-class life are directed towards young women. There is, for example, a more intense investment in marriage, motherhood and domestic life as a benchmark of successful femininity. This validates at least a retreat from the idea of combining full-time successful careers with motherhood, and it gives new, more professional, status to full-time mothers while opening up avenues for extensive media discussion of 'intensive mothering' and also for the creation of new markets (child-friendly coffee shops and so-called 'school-run fashion' for the so-called 'yummy mummies'). These markets also extend to push-chairs that double as jogging machines, sexy underwear ranges for pregnant women, new more fashion-oriented parenting magazines as well as a host of website organizations.[19] This professionalization of domestic life forcefully reverses the older feminist denunciation of housework as drudgery, and childcare as monotonous and never-ending, by elevating domestic skills and the bringing up of children as worthwhile and enjoyable. The well-run 'corporate family' endorses the 'intensification of mothering' as a mode of investment in the human capital of infants and children, while also countering any presumed loss of status on the part of the stay-at-home mother, who now directs her professional skills to ensure the unassailable middle-class status of her children. She will not be a complainer, nor will she be 'down among the women', as Fay Weldon (1971) darkly put it. Of course the assumption here, where stay-at-home mothers find sources of validation in the popular media, is that they have high-earning partners and so can afford to step out of the labour market. Within the prevailing logic of the new conservative feminism there is an expectation that such women will re-enter employment or become entrepreneurs for the reason that personal identity and middle-class status for women nowadays rest on occupation and economic activity and not solely on being a wife and mother.

Contemporary neoliberal discourse as it is addressed to young women (for example in the words of Sheryl Sandberg) emphasizes the importance of planning well for marriage and motherhood, and this now includes, in a gesture towards liberal feminism, finding the right kind of partner who will be prepared to consider his wife as an equal. The *dispositif* of new maternal-familialism is inextricably tied up with expansive norms of respectable middle-class life, which in turn entails careful financial planning, good self-governance to insure against family breakdown and, with the increasing professionalization of motherhood which sets new horizons for middle-class status on the basis of aspirational lifestyle, non-reliance on the state or on benefits and a female head of household who can 'do it all' even if she cannot quite 'have it all'. There is frequently some irony and feminist self-consciousness in the recounting of the rewards of good housekeeping. The UK popular press and television function as the debating chamber for these maternal transformations: the luminosities of visual culture show again and again, day in and day out, the triumph of the 'post baby body', or the favoured looks for the 'school run'. The modern woman is not 'that name' unless she is in possession of a well-dressed toddler or 'mini me'. We could go further and say that cultural intelligibility as a young woman is now tilted towards the achievement of 'affluent, middle-class maternity' with its many accoutrements, in particular a spectacularly slim body, a well-groomed and manicured appearance, and an equally attractive baby and husband. Motherhood no longer offers a short time-off period of respite from those forms of social power that comprise incitements and persuasions to get back in shape and to resume the work of achieving the highly sexualized body image which is now a hallmark of successful womanhood. Quite the opposite, in fact: as Jo Littler points out, the young mother must now avoid at all costs the danger of 'dowdiness' and this requires many hours of hard work in retaining her sexual desirability at all times (Littler 2013). It is almost too obvious to point out that the emphasis on vigilant attention to heteronormative desirability on the part of the wife and mother also functions to encourage marital fidelity and hence family stability. The wife is expected to remain highly desirable at all points in time during and after pregnancy, while (once again, just to stress the asymmetry of these norms) no such constant and repeated addresses are made to male partners. The 'post-feminist masquerade' of maternity reassures the social structures of domination by constraining young mothers in a field of anxieties brought about by the promise of 'complete perfection' (Riviere 1926; McRobbie 2008). This luminosity of contemporary femininity shines its light unsparingly: its significance stretches well beyond the pages of the women's magazines because at stake in these practices are matters of state, undertaken within the new moral economy of the family.

Visual-Media Governmentality, Maternity and 'Neoliberal Feminism'

With the evisceration of the public sector and the slimming down, to the point of extinction, of a range of family services, the requirement is that the family steps forward to look after itself and to inculcate the right kinds of self-responsibility in its children, while at the same time financially mopping up those costs that in the past would have been at least partially covered by the state. The middle-class family, as it was in the nineteenth century, becomes a more self-contained complex financial unit, requiring extensive lines of dependency and obligation in the form of loans, bequests, gifts and under-writing. This also accelerates processes of social polarization and class and racial divides to the detriment of those whose families cannot play this underwriting role. Additionally, there is a reversal of what Ulrich Beck wrote about in his theory of the reflexive modernization of Western societies, wherein contemporary individualization was made possible by the expansive welfarist undertakings of previous decades (in education, social services, public housing and employment benefits), which freed the young to make a life for themselves, often far away from the close ties of family and community associated with first modernity (Beck 1986). In contrast, and given the attention now paid to personal planning within the new gender-training regimes of contemporary femininity, it becomes incumbent once again on the professional mother to stage-manage and oversee the success of this kind of family enterprise. She is the new 'angel in the house', fulfilling what Donzelot attributed to the expert role of the middle-class mother in late nineteenth-century France. There is an insinu-ation echoing across the media that the feminist generation prioritized their own careers at the expense of their children, 'farming them out' to full-time nurseries.

Unsurprisingly there is no mention here of those women who cannot afford not to work, never mind the huge numbers of single-parent families where the mother is the sole breadwinner – such women as these make almost no appearance in the public debates that have taken place in recent years. This is also true of women from black and ethnic minority backgrounds, with the result that the discussion about maternity is almost wholly conducted by white women. Questions of the contemporary politics of black maternity, at least in the UK, remain largely invisible outside academia (Phoenix 1991). The emphasis that is placed during a recession on families being more responsible for themselves – more enterprising and more willing to take over the costs, which in times of more extensive social democratic government would have been covered by the state – thus becomes an important aspect of neoliberalism within the domestic sphere. So far, and in the chapters that follow, I will argue that this work of family responsibilization, at least in the UK, is entrusted to the feminine mass media and popular culture. As will also become apparent I will suggest that ultimately, in the UK, for low-income women, work and employment must take precedence over family.

By introducing the phrase 'visual-media governmentality', I want to conjoin the biopolitical model of governmentality developed by Foucault, with its attention to spaces, gazes, bodies, populations and the overseeing of conduct and activity, with the specific dimension of gender and media. In the first instance this would mean returning to Jacqueline Rose's psychoanalytic account of how the acquisition of femininity during girlhood is never fully achieved, and can always be somehow distracted from its point of fixity – a fact which in turn accounts for the wide range of regulative mechanisms put into place to ensure that normative femininity is indeed accomplished (Rose 1986). Rose's Lacanian account stresses processes of repetitive looking. The girl must be constantly looking at images that confirm her otherwise uncertain sense of self. Alongside this we could pose Judith Butler's queer theory of gender performativity in such a way that it does not supplant or negate Rose, but instead accents the crafting, scripting and repetitive inciting of gender norms as fictitious but institutionally embedded social practices, required so that heterosexual domination can be instated and maintained (Butler 1990). Femininity exists then as a seemingly fundamental and universal dividing practice, one which within the time and space of Western modernity has been constantly produced and reproduced by the various offices of the state and by the giant media corporations.

The history of girls' and women's magazines as social institutions, stands as a shining example of how femininity has been created as a seemingly distinctive separate space, one that charts the chronology of women's lives for them, while also punctuating the week or month with repetitive familiarity.[20] It is this format that is both expanded and more intensively visualized in the age of online communications. Instagram, Facebook, and the *Daily Mail's* 'Femail' section reproduce and in many ways replace the traditional format of the women's magazine, now available as a constant feed of images, updated hourly, and in recent times concentrating on pictures of glamorous and famous young women, either in stages of pregnancy or just after birth, when they are displaying their slim, 'toned' 'post-baby' bodies. Female viewers are invited into this mode of repetitive looking, well beyond the years of girlhood.

This landscape of power is intensified and made more complex in the age of digital and social media. The effect is compounded by the way in which neoliberal governmentality inserts itself firmly within the domestic sphere, eroding the previous boundaries of public and private, and of politics and entertainment, by establishing a site of cosy convergence, a politics of 'daytime TV' expressed, once again, during the Blair period in his preference for interviews conducted 'on the sofa'. Deleuze described the 'control of communications' as the most forceful modality of biopolitical power (Deleuze 1996). Within the spaces of contemporary communication, flows of gossip intersect with and coincide with matters of great urgency, to the point that the 'fun effect' often seriously compromises and detracts from questions of real gravity. Boundaries are eroded and moral confusion sets in. Political discourse cannot be separated from trivial comments about the appearance, age or sexual desirability of key protagonists. At the same time, the old-fashioned, more anonymous and formal modes of political engagement, such as those associated with the bureaucratic years of social democracy, where women often worked behind the scenes quietly pursuing a feminist agenda, are now replaced by the need to personalize all activities, put a name on and a face to everything one does, to monetize, gain publicity or followers and likes or dislikes in the full glare of the global media. To be effective requires going public, being constantly available and highly visible, and this in turn requires modes of self-branding and self-promotion that lessen the public service dimension of traditional political activity. There is no option it seems but to launch oneself into this sphere of entertainment if one wants to take part in public debate. Few aspects of everyday life and working life are now exempt from this requirement to self-promote. This has consequences for the more branded and personalized feminism that has surfaced in recent years and that comes immediately to be attached to certain names and careers. Feminists speaking out become immediately identifiable. Feminism is now a heavily named or signatured activity where, in the past, the 'collective' sufficed.

This is the context within which Sandberg's book *Lean In* was published, attracting enormous publicity across most of the quality press and television on the basis of her position as the Chief Operating Officer at Facebook in California (Sandberg 2012). Using the term lean-in as a rejoinder to women not to disconnect psychologically from work and from the career path at the point at which motherhood beckons, and more generally as a call to women in the workplace to position themselves close to those who are in leadership positions, so that they will be noticed, the book has given rise to so-called *Lean In* circles taking place in many US cities, a ghostly version of its more overtly feminist predecessor, the consciousness-raising group of the 1970s. Likewise, the TED talks Sandberg has given have attracted more than 2.4 million viewers on YouTube.[21] The singularity of Sandberg's account is that it brings an unashamedly feminist voice to a genre of writing that is associated with top US business schools and MBA courses, and which, despite the high status of such institutions, relies on a writing style that eschews conventional scholarship, or for that matter reportage, in favour of cheerful and uplifting anecdotes, helpful tips, homilies, sentimental eulogies to mentors and others who have helped the author in the course of her career, and name-dropping litanies of impressive friends and acquaintances within the ranks of the rich and powerful; all of which is set within a format that carefully avoids saying anything mildly critical of, or detrimental to, her employer.

The adoption of the business manual format is certainly almost risible from the perspective of most women who would define themselves as feminist and who have taken part in any form of feminist politics over the years; and this accounted for the hostile or dismissive reviews of the book that appeared in liberal newspapers such as the *Guardian* and other similar newspapers and online sites across the world.

The simple use of a vocabulary drawn from the world of business and then applied, not just to how women can do better in the world of work, but also in home life, suggests the extent to which corporate values have achieved a fundamental centrality and seemingly incontestable as well as uncontroversial status. Where in the past almost all strains of feminism, including liberal feminism, would have found just cause to challenge the culture of the male-dominated business world, in Sandberg's case this no longer holds. From her perspective, feminism means finding better ways of adjusting to this business culture, not trying to change it, and when change is proposed it must always also be good for business, at least insofar as it extracts better performance from the workforce. The most significant point the book makes is that women in the organizations for which Sandberg has worked, no matter how well qualified, tend to anticipate the difficulties they will encounter when they have children by detaching from their job in advance of the time at which they become pregnant and then have some time off (though barely more than a few weeks in the US). In doing so women needlessly jeopardize their chances for regaining their roles and promotional prospects, where, with greater confidence and self-belief, they could somehow manage the transition to combining work and motherhood. Sandberg argues then for 'leaning in', and this in turn becomes a wider metaphor for women who, in the context of corporate life, still show signs of insecurity and lack of confidence. Much of the book repeats the early feminist observations, cast in terms of a social psychology of gender, where women fear disapproval or fear being seen as aggressive and unfeminine because they want to be liked. Instead of homing in on the rituals of male corporate bonding and the deep-rooted sexism that thrives on stereotypes about 'scary women', Sandberg's advice is typically to find ways of outmanoeuvring these obstacles through such (gender-conforming) strategies as smiling, while also 'staying focused'. Her own career, in which she began at Harvard before working her way through some of the key companies and organizations in the US, including the World Bank, the US Treasury, McKinsey, Google and then Facebook, means that she is now one of the most powerful (and well-paid) businesswomen in the US, if not in the world. What she counsels other women to do is to learn how to play the corporate game more deftly. This may mean being willing to take on new challenges rather than saying 'I'm not ready'; it will also mean being willing to re-enter the labour market after a period out for children, at a lower scale, on the basis that this can then be a stepping stone for regaining the status or pay-point lost on taking time out.

Sandberg shows her liberal feminist credentials by describing her own modest background and the sheer hard work and long hours she put in to make her way to the top. Prior to having children she routinely did more than fourteen-hour days in the office and, even though she also learnt how to be more productive on fewer hours in the workplace following motherhood, she repeatedly talks about how she still returns to the laptop after reading her children their bedtime stories. She insists that children do not suffer from having a hard-working mother, she admits to 'feeling sad' when she doesn't see enough of her kids; and she makes the point that she does her best to get home in time for the evening meal (though she does not mention the routines of shopping, cooking and clearing up, so the reader can only infer she has staff). Having 'good help' is essential, and she is also in the fortunate position of having extended family close by in the same neighbourhood. She counsels women to look for the right kind of husband who will willingly share the housework and childcare, and she also suggests bringing 'negotiating strategies' to the marriage and home front when it comes to trying to find a way to combine successful motherhood with 'workplace success'. The liberal feminist message delivered to the heartland of this neoliberal world is that women can continue to be economically active, and highly successful, during the early years of having children. They need not lose out as long as they learn how to 'lean in'.

The words 'day care', never mind 'state provided nurseries', do not appear across the pages of the book. Sandberg's tone is positive, cheerful, uplifting and wholeheartedly feminist in that she earnestly wants to improve women's lives. But there is a whole vocabulary that describes the world of non-elite employment which is totally missing from her writing: this includes such words as poverty and unemployment, the high cost and often low quality of childcare, the reliance of white middle-class elite women on the low-paid domestic labour of migrant women (many of whom will be separated from their own children in order to earn a living and hence unable themselves to provide 'quality parenting') and so on. Nothing at all is said about the non-existence of paid maternity leave for women in the US, or about the need for employer-provided crèches and nurseries, as if that would be a step too far in the direction of criticism of corporate culture and the business world. Sandberg does not even suggest local neighbourhood, or self-help nursery care; instead there is a doggedness about putting in the long hours and working one's way up the corporate ladder. Implicitly Sandberg is talking to young women like herself, who are attending prestigious universities. This means her address is exclusively to a privileged, largely white, middle-class sector of the population. What Sandberg describes as feminist she also inaugurates as a comfortable neoliberal feminism, a political force that is defined in such terms as to protect and enhance the already existing privileges of a relatively select sector of the female population, whose position, especially as they enter into motherhood, is now charged with even greater moral responsibility than before, in times of withdrawal of the state and reduction in all public spending. This is a radically de-politicized and accommodating feminism, and its conservatism is most apparent in its shying away from argument and confrontation. It merely requests a place at the table. This, then, has emerged as the public face of neoliberal feminism. Sandberg herself has stayed close to power since her earliest days at university, becoming the research assistant and later close friend of former Chief Treasurer Larry Summers. Her narrative, sprinkled as it is with personal biographical details, can be seen also as a kind of answer to the question implicitly posed by *Revolutionary*

Road and by Betty Friedan as the 'problem with no name'. By proudly reclaiming the word feminism and bringing it back into use in the world of business as well as in the home after a long period during which it was cast aside as irrelevant or no longer needed, Sandberg also reinvents liberal feminism, an American formation, so that it even more fully complies with the values of the corporate environment.

A new maternal–feminine performs a double function for the neoliberal hegemony of the present. By endorsing and extending liberal feminist principles it provides the centre right and the centre left with a more up-to-date way of engaging with women and women's issues, while simultaneously it expunges from popular memory the values of the radical and social democratic tradition, which had forged such a close connection with feminism through the pursuit of equality and collective provision for families. What this strenuous ideological activity forecloses and seeks to forget is the very possibility of socialized childcare, including after-school care, youth clubs and publicly provided leisure facilities as a social investment and a public good. The bombardment of images showing super-wealthy mothers enjoying their luxury lifestyles introduces new forms of consumer hedonism into the hard work of motherhood, distracting attention away from what feminists in the past named as drudgery and chores. This palliative effect even in its trickle-down version, involving routines of play dates, coffee shops and jogging buggies, reinstates new norms of middle-class hegemony against which less advantaged families can only feel themselves to be inferior or inadequate, or else condemned for not having tried hard enough. What was in the Victorian era a moral high ground of imperialist maternal citizenship is now recast as a no-less-moralistic playground of lifestyle and consumer culture, predicated on young women making the right choices and adopting, at an early age, the right kind of life-plan. Overall there is an attempt to consolidate the power and dominance of a newly inflected middle-class and white ideal of maternity and family life by means of a repertoire of values established within various discourses that converge and become identifiable as a form of 'visual media governmentality'. This also permits new ideas of conservative feminism to rise to the surface, ideas which borrow heavily from the liberal feminism of the past in order to create the contours for a neoliberal leadership-feminism predicated on preserving class and racial privilege through the prism of a normative femininity – one which legitimates punitive measures against those women who for good historical reasons do not possess what is needed to move up the meritocratic ladder of opportunity, which also functions as a substitute for a now derelict and denuded idea of universal welfare (Littler 2017). The new familialism, with all of its blogging glamorization of maternity, is anti-feminist because what disappears over the horizon in terms of public discourse is the possibility of state funding for full-time nursery care, and for pre-school and after-school provision, along the lines embarked upon decades ago by social democratic governments in Scandinavia. Instead, the private solutions that must be found, such as live-in nannies, are available only for the tiny percentage of already high-flying corporate women, for whom feminism is simply synonymous with female ambition.

2
Feminism and the Politics of Resilience

The Profit from Feminism?

What are the mechanisms by which some notional idea of feminism is adopted, taken up and made compatible with the needs and expectations of consumer capitalism as it has historically directed itself towards women within a frame of normative femininity?[1] How is feminism mainstreamed? How does the feminist impact of the #MeToo period come to be translated into the heartland of gendered popular culture? There is no shortage of contemporary examples, from the Dior t-shirt 'We Should All Be Feminists' to pop singer Beyoncé's famous backdrop showing the word FEMINIST, to the *Stylist* magazine, encouraging its readers to meet up at the Women's March in London (Saturday 19 January 2019). I will focus in this chapter on three interconnected elements which arguably do some of this translation work. These are the 'perfect', which appertains to lifestyle and the terrain of the feminine 'good life'; the 'imperfect', which offers some scope (but within carefully demarcated boundaries) for criticism of and divergence from these ideals; and finally 'resilience', which becomes the favoured tool and therapeutic instrument for recovery and repair.

In the last few years a number of key feminist scholars have also found themselves responding to this process of feminist mainstreaming. Sarah Banet-Weiser, for example, has, over a longer period of time, debated the politics of 'commodity feminism' (Mukherjee and Banet-Weiser 2012). She, along with others, has also referred to the currents of popular feminism where the new age of activism is registered and, through a complicated set of moves, is incorporated into the high-visibility spaces of media and mass culture (Banet-Weiser 2018; Bull and Allen 2018; Allen and Bull 2018; Gill and Orgad 2018; Rottenberg 2018; James 2015). Each of these interrelated terms – 'perfect-imperfect-resilience' (*p-i-r*) – prompts actions that address the challenge posed by a new age of feminism. They comprise a *dispositif* for the management of emerging feminisms. They grab hold of its flows and expressions and pull them into a less disconcerting agenda for change. They follow on from and replace the de-politicizing post-feminist ethos of female individualism (circa 1997–2007), where feminism was shunned as old and no longer needed, with something that resonates more comfortably with the new climate of political awareness on gender inequalities (McRobbie 2008). Feminism can now be accommodated and recognized as socially relevant, and in this respect it comes forward as a force that will occasion new modes of governmentality. The logistics of this process, moving from a resistance movement to something that can be not only accommodated, but also managed, controlled and then possessed as a source of ideas and innovation, is flagged up as vital to understanding what is at stake in the new feminisms of recent years.

The perfect is also a class category, which is now bolstered by a feminist underpinning. It is driven by competition, which operates to preserve privilege, to designate an area of aspirational lifestyle defined by 'having it all', while both describing and marking out a largely white and upper-middle-class sector of women epitomized by COO Facebook and feminist Sheryl Sandberg.[2] There is a kind of invitation-only dynamic issued to black women and women of colour, something which will be considered through the course of this chapter. The function of the perfect is to encourage women to succeed meritocratically, while simultaneously introducing heightened competition, constantly redifferentiating and establishing division, resulting in a feminism that is infinitely divided and gradated, defining ways of living that can also be compatible with what were originally the aims of liberal feminism and are now more closely articulated to what we might call neoliberal 'leadership-feminism' (Littler 2017; and see also Rottenberg 2018). Following on from this, the imperfect is a response to the unviability of the emphasis on success, and it too relies on a feminist voice, this time to engage with the idea of failure, while also drawing tight lines around those terrains of experience where it is possible to fail, where flaws can be entertained. This means that the imperfect is in a binary relation to the perfect, with both exhibiting boundary-marking and highly regulative dimensions. Though with a much longer history in clinical psychology, the idea of resilience springs into existence as a 'bounce-back' mechanism, finding expression across a whole terrain of popular culture (Rose and Lentzos 2015; Bracke 2016; Gill and Orgad 2018). Robin James pays attention to female pop musicians, in particular Lady Gaga and Beyoncé, each of whom professes to damage having been done – damage figured as constitutive of their wounded womanhood – but where, again within specific parameters, there is the possibility for recovery. In contrast Rihanna, who James also subjects to analytic scrutiny, shows some resistance to resilience by means of what James labels melancholy (James 2015).

In the pages that follow I pose questions as to the working of this set of terms (*p-i-r*) in their reciprocal entanglements. Is commercially endorsed feminism here being shaped up and deployed to replenish contemporary capitalism, as Boltanski and Chiapello (2005) argue in relation to prior social movements? If so, how can we gauge and make sense of the profitability of this feminism? What do we make of the rise of various empowerment feminisms as commercial ventures, some offering fitness and resilience training, others taking the form of self-help manuals, online tutorials and YouTube seminars (Banet-Weiser 2018)?

On 19 September 2018 one of the headlines in the right-wing newspaper the *Daily Mail* ran 'Terrible Toll of the Pressure to Be Perfect'. The article reported on the work of psychologist Nancy Tucker, who told of her own mental health struggles, including serious eating disorders springing from a variety of factors such as the pressures of academic achievement, being phobic about failure, the constant comparing of oneself to others and the overall experience of growing up as a girl in the 'striving culture'. Tucker refers to the reports published recently suggesting that 26 per cent of young women between the ages of sixteen and twenty-four report mental health problems and that girls from the age of six upwards seem prone to self-berating for fear of being 'average' or 'ordinary', when at school they are being told to 'reach for the stars'. In this kind of public debate carried out on the pages of a tabloid newspaper, a correlation is drawn between the idea of the perfect and high rates of mental ill health among teenage girls. Predicated on intense competition and focusing inevitably on the lives of female celebrities or the already well-off and successful, the perfect is a force for generating such powerful feelings of division, isolation and failure among those who appear to be within its direct field of address (e.g. the middle-England daughters of *Daily Mail* readers) that damage is accrued. What makes the perfect distinctive in recent years is that it emboldens itself with a feminist message, as if success is a kind of feminist duty to oneself and for the sake of other women, a new or emergent form of gendered citizenship (Kanai 2017).[3] The perfect delineates success for women, with feminism providing a moral imperative. The perfect (with this feminist strand) binds women tightly to something that causes them pain, thus acting as a form of what Berlant calls 'cruel optimism' (Berlant 2011).

We can trace a direct link through contemporary popular culture, from the extolling of the fantasy of the perfect life as a horizon for female happiness, to a range of shows (e.g. the hit TV HBO series *Girls*) that also now bear a feminist imprint and that voice dissatisfaction with the ideal of perfection, instead asserting the need to embrace the imperfect. From here there is another strand of work that acknowledges the damage done by the perfect, but which looks to repair and recovery through the idea of resilience. A variety of modes of story-telling and testimony-giving as to the realm of suffering experienced, and to what is required in terms of inner strength to achieve a life worth living, now underscore so many commercial feminine and also putatively feminist undertakings. Celebrities pour out their sorrows and their tragedies as if the act of telling is cathartically part of the process of recovery. The seemingly feminist aim here is that of sharing the story, so as to empower other women. In so many cases the celebrity has achieved success while also dealing with much pain. It is as if the adversity becomes the mechanism for further effort and determination to succeed. This, as Robin James shows, then becomes an individually scripted but now shared pathway to resilience and recovery.

Does this, to put it crudely, prepare women to expect the adversity of gender inequality and get used to the toll it takes, on the basis that with particular kinds of strivings undertaken, as demonstrated by celebrities like Lady Gaga or Lena Dunham, hardship or suffering can eventually be 'overcome'?[4] What does it mean when this entanglement of elements comes to be taken as a kind of truth of the self? Could we also see this as one among many strategies to stabilize gender and, in this case, femininity at a point in time when there is so much disruption of, and so many challenges to, the binary gender regime? Does the '*p-i-r*' protect the status quo by permitting some ideas of feminism to circulate, as if to give young women a helping hand? Is it not also the case that a good deal is invested here in maintaining a prevailing definition of selfhood/girlhood, propped up precisely by this configuring of perfect and imperfect to which is then added the further support of resilience training? Is resilience predicated on a withdrawal of social care, in the broadest sense, indeed even that form of care provided in a previous era by the state (pastoral teachers, youth workers, adolescent counsellors, etc.), which in turn gives rise to a new kind of eviscerated gendered social contract, one which can seek some degree of legitimacy by inscribing within itself a smattering of feminist ideals? This would mark out the contours of a model of self-governance by means of access to these *p-i-r* provisions. And feminism becomes part of the official pedagogy for resilience-training. Make women stronger, independent and more resilient, so that they can better look after themselves? Inculcate competition through so many appeals for women to assume leadership, so as to engender self-responsibilization (a clumsy term, but one which is indicative of the aim of making people able to pay their own way)? If this is all correct, then we can pinpoint resilience-training as a category of high political consequence, one which marks a key moment of change.

Competitive Femininity

If neoliberalism promotes enterprise and competition with a specific address to the individual's capacity to be self-responsible, then the question arises as to how to inculcate such a competitive ethos among women who might previously have been exposed to different value systems, for example as nurturers, home-makers, teachers and carers – in short, as women who were willing to subordinate their career ambitions to fit with family life. Or in times of feminist activism, as women who were committed to working with less privileged others, devoting time to activities aimed at improving facilities and resources that would benefit all. Post-war social democracy in the UK offered women opportunities in the caring professions, often within the public sector, in health services, teaching, social work, in childcare, local government etc. It was only with the rise of the New Public Management (considered in more depth in the chapter that follows) that the free market and competition came to be a driving force in these sectors. How then does neoliberalism replace ideas of public service with audits and competitive tendering? How is the female care-giving ethos reversed and replaced with the pursuit of 'excellence'? How can young women be trained more thoroughly to compete? If feminism has re-entered the popular imagination can it be corralled so as to assist in this transformation? Can feminism even be relied upon to encourage young women to be more individualistic, more entrepreneurial, and might this be its value to contemporary capitalism, as a social critique (Boltanski and Chiapello 2005)? This is where, unsurprisingly perhaps, two forces step forward, both of which have historically dedicated themselves to the social reproduction of the gender regime, these being education and consumer culture. These are affordances, points of offering where contemporary feminism is made into an availability-as-critique.

In consumer culture we find a clustering of themes which focus around female success, in work, in family life, in self and in body. There is a distinctive genre shift reflected across the editorials of the leading magazines. A more serious note is struck, especially with regard to work and employment. There is a more emphatic ideal of the perfect that is articulated where female fantasy is entwined with lifestyle, and where competition is energetically pursued as an inner-directed compulsion. This is not just self-improvement or make-over culture, but a competition with and against the self to achieve those landmarks that are linked to the perfect.[5] The right job is nothing without a perfectly sculpted body. There is also the Fitbit wristband telling you how well you have done today. The perfect marks out the contours of female competition as inscribed within the mundane features of everyday life. It informs and shapes particular forms of popular media. It is not just about the body beautiful, but also about being able to follow recipes and prepare and serve beautiful-looking food, laid on a well-set table, with candles and with distinctive and stylish dinnerware. These are the accessories that enhance one's own desirability, making one more eligible on the marriage and relationship market. Even the most mundane free magazines provided by stores like Tesco or Waitrose endorse the perfect, transcribed into the popular aesthetics of colourful and appealing healthy eating. When they are addressing a readership of mothers there are typically pages in these magazines devoted to preparing picturesque lunchboxes – 'one your kids will love and one for you too' (*Tesco Magazine*, September 2018). Competitive femininity here finds itself at home in the domestic sphere: the young working mother, getting up at 5 a.m. for her work-out,[6] preparing healthy breakfasts for the children with help from her feminist-friendly husband, heading off to work while also scheduling in a hair appointment at lunchtime, remembering to do some 'batch cooking' in the evening, mindful of the need to 'be calmer and more contented' with 'random acts of self-kindness' (*Tesco Magazine*, September 2018). This new 'angel in the house' will also aim to be the first woman 'on the management board', and in this format the perfect-feminine relies on an inner-directed compulsion to compete with herself, in order to exude an exemplary mode of feminist leadership. She will be a role model for friends and younger colleagues and yet also 'find time' for herself. When there is an interpellation effect to black and Asian women to join the ranks of this new feminist-styled 'angel in the house', we might ponder the boundary-marking strategies being employed through vectors of race and ethnicity.[7] What Banet-Weiser refers to as an 'economy of visibility' demarcates the simple presence of more black models and personalities in this media field as a gesture to diversity politics, while at the same time there is a sense in which black and Asian women are now welcomed as if an invitation has been issued, one which also contains a conditionality (Banet-Weiser 2018). The black or Asian woman must exude a sense of happiness at just being there, in such good company (Kanai 2018; Ahmed 2010).

If this wider sphere denotes the invitational spread of the perfect, simultaneously present is also an allocated space for its critique. Imperfection is announced as a corrective to the pressure young women 'put themselves under', as the phrase goes. The perfect as a technology of the self therefore displays a capacity for reflexivity. The imperfect warrants further new forms of 'care of the self', while also being a space where feminism can be openly avowed; for example, in anger and frustration about harassment in the workplace and misogyny in the street, in fat shaming or in sexism in advertising. In this way the discourses of the imperfect legitimate, even more fully than does the perfect, the presence of feminism. They slide into place more seamlessly. Discourses proliferate saying that imperfections are to be expected, that they allow us to 'embrace' who we are. Women can thrive, if not warts and all, at least flaws and all. 'Love your imperfections' is shouted to women from so many billboards. We can trace the passage in popular culture of the two interwoven ideals, the perfect and the imperfect, devices, routine 'technologies of the self', but at the same time socially divisive, pathological, injurious norms of quiescent, predominantly white middle-classness.[8] The perfect extols a vision of life that foregrounds an array of well-groomed bodies, beautiful spaces, tasteful things and exciting identities, which indicate a sense of belonging within a comfortable family and consumer-oriented milieu. The idea of the perfect hinges on a fantasy of middle-class futurity.

Though they may dream quietly of Berlant's 'good life', the idea of the perfect is not so openly avowed by working-class women across the boundaries of ethnicity, for the obvious reason that there is a barrier effect and violent intent underpinning this configuration of perfect lives (Berlant 2008). As a status marker the perfect allows 'neoliberal feminists' to maintain their privilege by differentiating themselves from others. The perfect invites envy and competition, while also providing role models for those lower down the social ladder. The message is to aspire but also to know your place. The debate in the quality US press about 'having it all', considered in detail by Catherine Rottenberg (2018), could also be seen in this light. How does the neoliberal feminism she names animate itself by constantly drawing class and ethnicity boundaries, pulling away and separating itself off from other more inclusive and egalitarian new feminisms? What Rottenberg labels neoliberal feminism marks itself off from other new feminisms through this invocation of the perfect. The very idea of 'having it all' is an expression of upper-middle-class white identity: to express such a desire is to be potentially within reach of fulfilling such an ambition. It envisages the level of prosperity needed to be able to 'pencil in' jogging and the gym alongside the top job, employing a nanny or at least an au pair, spending time with the children, while also maintaining a wide circle of friends as well as a good relationship with husband or partner.[9] The accoutrements of 'having it all' fold neatly into the idea of the perfect. That is to say, the expression 'having it all' also has an aggressive intent: it is a boundary-marking exercise designed to ward off and belittle those for whom it cannot possibly apply. The perfect points to a way of organizing one's life as an affluent woman where certain heteronormative life-cycle stages can be met and celebrated. But it is not as though poor or disadvantaged women are simply shunned, and pushed out of the picture. This is not how the boundary-marking activity works. The logic of 'cruel optimism' within both traditional (i.e. from the rags-to-riches days of Hollywood weepies and melodrama) and now seemingly feminist-informed feminine mass culture, is to embrace the idea of a gender meritocracy.

The perfect also takes root and flourishes within the frame of the gaining of qualifications. This is where the educational apparatuses have a role to play. These subjects of the perfect are typically not just educated to degree level, but have graduated from a so-called top university. When university education becomes an asset in the portfolio logic of the perfect, it too comes to possess a violent underpinning, demeaning those girls for example who are only able to consider a local or poorly rated university. The perfect in this context articulates with those changes that have taken place in schools and in universities over the last decades – changes that have made them spaces for young women, spheres of so-called excellence, where success is actively promoted. Such meritocratic possibilities, which in reality portend only widening inequalities for women disadvantaged by class and race, come to the attention of their aspirational and middle-class recipients cloaked in the language of the New Public Management, which foregrounds measurable goals, individual performance, competition, and extensive self-monitoring. Good parenting also means supporting girls to achieve excellence. Doing well at school and going to a 'top' university have become badges of female success. A dividing line is drawn marking out those young women who are able to stay within the school and higher education system and those who fall below this line. We can see then how the worlds of education and of consumer culture come into play, articulating with the ideas of the new popular feminism, modifying their own provisions while also attempting to take control of this force for change. Women's magazines such as *Elle* and *Grazia* champion much more professional jobs for women than they did in the past.[10] They also run features celebrating any number of feminist heroines, from Jane Austen to the suffragettes to Frida Kahlo. A detailed study of these magazines over the last few years would show a very different landscape from the staple fare of the preceding period.

New forms of feminist activism have created a wave of political awareness, protest and determination to challenge gender inequality. The *p-i-r* inserts itself within this fast-moving space, tempering its agenda for sexual justice by proposing a set of values more accommodating to contemporary capitalism. The aspiration towards a high-paying job through gaining the right qualifications also promises access

to consumer culture, which in turn permits further permu-
tations of female competition and status differentiation.
Consumer culture, especially the world of women's fashion,
beauty and media genres, remains part of a 'magic system'
(Williams 1960). Following Boltanski and Chiapello it may
well be that by these means a feminist critique of society is
absorbed so as to renew or replenish the capitalist economy.
This would be to propose feminism as a potential source of
innovation. But before we could take this further, some key
sociological questions would need to be asked. What kind of
'feminism' is produced from within these popular genres, and
how is it received or responded to by readers and viewers?[11]
And in fields dictated by fashion trends and fast turnovers,
in what ways can and cannot popular feminism endure?
At what point does it come up against its limits? Where
and when within the immensely profitable fashion-beauty
complex will the plugs be pulled on the seemingly unstop-
pable wave of new feminist interventions? At what point
must it be stifled or cut down to size?[12]

  The feminine-perfect is a *dispositif* of contemporary
biopolitics, operating almost continually at the everyday
level of social media and popular culture, inserting itself
within the localized and privatized spaces of young women's
lives, making them from an early age such fretful creatures,
worried about their bodies, worried about their exams.
This is to say that the perfect carries violent intent not just
in its racial and class-based exclusionary effect but also in
its acts of inclusion, for those directly within its embrace.
Because they have been given a lift up, because they have
become 'subjects of attention', these aspirational young
women are encouraged to feel they ought to be even better.
With body and self seemingly folded into each other, they
become subjects of chronic anxiety. There are so many young
women committing suicide as young as twelve or thirteen.
Often a grieving parent will say that their daughter had been
bullied at school or left out of things, for not being pretty
enough, or that she had thought herself ugly, even though
the accompanying Instagram photographs show this to be
far from the case. (I often ask myself how parents are able to
bear this terrible loss when it seems tied to the fleeting and
capricious cruelties of growing up, when a young person's

self-perception or the views of her friends and classmates are subject to such fluctuation from day to day, if not from hour to hour?)[13] We read almost on a daily basis the findings of academic researchers across the world; for example that 25 per cent of teenage girls in the UK are 'clinically depressed'.[14]

Is this a moral panic that amplifies the phenomenon, so that mental ill health becomes a kind of gathering point, an umbrella, a label, platform and point of identification for young women today? Has there been recently a tendency to over-clinicalize symptoms that pertain to social circumstances, to Instagram culture and the terms and conditions of the beauty-fashion complex? Headteachers write articles or give public talks about how to stave off depression, how to build 'resilience'. Aware of the unhealthily high standards to which many young women subject themselves (as they compete against themselves), teachers then find ways of challenging the tyranny of the perfect, telling pupils not to worry, while also encouraging them to embrace their flaws. These interwoven pathologies of the perfect with its seeming corrective, the imperfect, thus function simultaneously: they are the means by which young female subjects recognize themselves. They become ways of making sense of the gendered world in its current inception. They solidify into recognizable modes of subjectivity, forms of 'character', inviting young women to identify, to say 'yes this is me'. There is an assumption then of a sovereign self and the need for self-responsibility that comes with it. On the one hand, the *p-i-r* appears to speak most directly to young white middle-class women, on the other hand it has the capacity to reach much further. What is observable in the world of feminine popular culture is the variety of voices, statements, recommendations and advice which seem to spring into being as if directly in response to the troubles of the perfect. The purpose of my argument below, where I pay some attention to just two of these iterations, is neither to make any precise claims as to their power and influence, nor about their representativeness, but rather to assert their place in this cluttered familiar landscape of feminine ephemera. In each case there is a sense of urgency, even crisis, invoked, which is what gives to the idea of resilience its value, relevance and applicability to young women today. Resilience marks the therapeutic space which comes to

dominate discourses of both popular media and public health
as they come into play around question of young people, and
in this case young women and mental health today.

The Politics of Resilience

In Brené Brown's book *The Gifts of Imperfection*, a young
woman, being persuaded of the therapeutic value of acknowl-
edging one's imperfections, is reported as having asked
'What if my friends/family/co-workers like the perfect me
better ...?' (Brown 2010, p. 51). Trained in psychology
and social work, Brown, whose entrepreneurial activities
include a blog, online tutorials as well as various books and
articles, exemplifies the self-help genre specializing in dealing
with shame, and more recently with the harm done by the
pressures of the perfect. Indeed, the three terms 'perfect-
imperfect-resilience' mark precisely the terrain marked out
in this book by Brown. That it is a *New York Times* best-
seller testifies to its wide appeal as a pop psychology volume.
Brown dwells on a range of affects, feelings and emotions
that have harmful effects. The great majority of those she
interviews are female, and typically they are busy mothers
and wives. With a strong focus on the individual and not at
all on the wider socio-political environment, she highlights
shame as a painful feeling 'or experience that we are flawed
and unworthy'. This can include being shown up for having
an untidy house, giving a public talk that goes badly, having
an unkempt appearance in a public place, having an unflat-
tering photograph seen by strangers, or simply feeling oneself
to be not good enough. Such experiences can be dealt with,
however, with the aid of the various techniques described
by Brown as 'shame resilience'. Talking about the painful
experience and 'moving through it' helps the individual to
develop the courage needed to acknowledge one's imperfections. As a familiar part of the self-help genre, Brown
offers tips – often in the form of acronyms – such as DIG
(get deliberate, get inspired, go). The emphasis on taking
practical steps can reveal, she suggests, that there are indeed
gifts to be found in our imperfections. 'Shame', she writes,

'is the birthplace of perfectionism', and this in turn gives rise to so many pathologies, including depression and even addiction. Perfectionism, she argues, rests on the misplaced belief that through sheer effort it is possible to shield oneself from pain. But, she continues, pursuing the idea of a perfect life backfires; it exacerbates rather than overcomes vulnerability; it intensifies pain. A first step in resilience-training is to learn to embrace imperfection and with it find the value of self-compassion and ultimately achieve a stronger sense of self-worth. The idea is to stop comparing the self with others, embrace one's own imperfections, learn how to 'tolerate disappointment', see the value of asking for help, and finally find a pathway to self-protection.

This is a conservative response to the pathologies of the perfect, which according to Brown comprises an inner-directed drive to be seen in a favourable light by others. Female subjects of the perfect suffer from a rather nebulous set of difficulties, inevitably worries about body image and anxieties about parenting, being too busy and distracted to find a way of being true to the self. The author refers to her own experience of breakdown, addiction, recovery and being a parent. She makes the point that her own struggles were not so terrible, her drinking did not lead her to 'bottom out', her partying was just something she wanted to curb when she completed her Masters degree. Brown mentions that she and her partner have sought to scale back their professional careers so as to concentrate more on time with children and on enjoyable creative activities. Material success, she is implying, is not a guarantee for a happy life. Writing in a plain style, Brown urges women to be kind to themselves. Resilience has a role to play in helping young people to tolerate disappointment, and not to expect too much success, too much love and happiness, too much approval by others at all times. The author refers to the several occasions in which she dropped out of education, graduating only at the age of 29. She does not therefore embody success in the corporate leadership style associated with most people who give TED talks. She is a modest, somewhat reluctant or retiring celebrity, who nevertheless assembles these elements as part of a carefully cultivated brand identity. Even with a PhD to her name, the author does not present herself as unambiguously successful, and to this extent she embodies the 'ordinary' values she advocates, and which can be learnt with resilience technique and by embracing one's flaws. She preaches an ethos that it is fine for women just to be 'OK', and this means being a 'good enough' mum, not trying to have the perfect body, keeping workloads manageable and not all-encompassing, and making family life a priority. Resilience is deployed here to reinforce the pro-family stance of the work–life balance. Resilience techniques help women to step back from hard-edged leadership-feminism, thereby finding self-esteem as a woman without being pressured or 'bullied' by the perfect.

Red and Resilience

By tracking what seems like a shift from liberal to neoliberal feminism and back again, with the former proving itself more enduring perhaps, we can throw some light on a set of tensions and uncertainties as to how the current new forms of feminist activism will register across the social field and in particular in consumer culture. We have hypothesized that the *p-i-r* plays an important role, by providing a vocabulary which addresses current issues that stem from women's historic subjugation without aiming to dismantle or even profoundly disrupt the prevailing gender regime. We could see the *p-i-r* as managing change in the light of the new feminist activism. The *p-i-r* is a cultural–therapeutic formation independent of, but in articulation with, what I have referred to as neoliberal leadership-feminism and its predecessor liberal feminism. Of course, from the perspective of the UK there arises a question as to the precise political valency of the popular feminism to which the *p-i-r* reacts. This is a much bigger question than can be answered here.[15] Instead, we can take the investigation a little further by looking now at *Red*, which is one of the UK's leading middle-market women's magazines aimed at women from their late twenties to early forties. The October 2018 edition celebrated *Red*'s twentieth birthday, thus providing a useful window to assess changes in the magazine and its readership. The point here is not to claim any kind of representative status for this particular magazine, nor to provide a detailed textual analysis. My aim is simply to draw out some recurrent features. Does the *p-i-r* find a place within this commercial landscape? Does feminism also find itself spoken of, and thus spoken into being? Does the magazine herald, and pronounce, and thus play some role in producing the feminism of which it talks? The readership here appears to be young adult women who are either on the cusp of settling down with a partner, who are single, working and aiming to find a partner, or who are already embarked on family life and 'juggling' with small children, a partner and a career. With a strong emphasis on the world of fashion and beauty products, the demographic is middle class: aspirational but not wealthy. We can read the finer details of this target market through the precise array of advertisements, the fashion and beauty edits, the lifestyle products, the travel features and so on, all of which must be deemed affordable, though of course also impregnated with elements of desire and fantasy (Sophia Coppola's Belize holiday home). Most significant of all is the presence across so many pages of non-white models, celebrities and others. *Red* is by no means alone in the magazine world in showing that it embraces diversity, having been faced with such vocal criticism from women of colour in recent times. Black, Asian and mixed-race women are featured throughout (announced on the front page are features on Corinne Bailey Rae, Joan Armatrading, Amma Asante and Mishal Husain). From the opening editorial page black models are more immediately prominent. And the first beauty product advertisement on page 11 features foundation for black as well as white skin (Clinique). The mode of insertion of women of colour into this domain of popular culture goes beyond what Ahmed would describe as 'happy diversity'; indeed it is celebratory diversity (Ahmed 2012). The BAME participants must display no anger about past exclusions. The fact that this is a birthday issue means that the magazine itself is in celebratory mode, reflecting on its own history and changes. In this issue of *Red* the line which runs through the various features (mostly interviews with a range of well-known and successful women in media, arts, business and other professional careers) is the encouragement to women to enjoy more ordinary pleasures and not to put oneself under too much pressure. It is then the job of these successful women to act as role models and disenchant readers as to the illusory nature of Hollywood fame and celebrity lifestyle, without depriving them of fantasies of beauty, happiness, romance and pleasure. What can be seen through the magazine is a sense of vacillation and uncertainty as to how to steer a pathway that absorbs some of the black feminist critique about the absence of black women, and which seems to listen to discontents about the over-emphasis on the perfect body and perfect life, while at the same time keeping intact the fantasies of femininity which of course connect with the products and fashions being featured and which provide the advertising revenue on which the whole enterprise relies.

One way of doing this is to foreground a specific type of celebrity who is able to demonstrate both qualities simultaneously, i.e. she both lives the dream and she debunks the pleasures, drawing attention to her own imperfections and to her reliance on some of the therapeutic techniques of resilience. This contradiction is vividly realized on the front cover, which shows a full body shot of the white, blonde television presenter Fearne Cotton (married to the son of Rolling Stones guitarist Ronnie Wood) in a pink tulle evening dress/girlish party 'frock', standing on a balcony with the Eiffel Tower in the background. This is not however an austere *Vogue*-type photograph, but rather shows Cotton in a natural pose, with a hand on the balcony rail, smiling widely. It is hardly an innocent choice for a cover picture, given how widely publicized was the feminist-led 'pink stinks' campaign of a few years back and more recently the activism and event staged at the TopShop store on Oxford Street by young feminists to publicize a book titled *Feminists Don't Wear Pink*.[16] *Red* magazine is aimed at an older readership but nevertheless it has to manage a pathway which above all else keeps its advertisers on board, since without this revenue its future would be in jeopardy. So as to leave no one in doubt, a pink tulle floor-length ball gown comes to the rescue. Tucked inside and concentrated in the features section, in interviews with various well-known women (Fearne Cotton again, and actor Emma Thompson), one single theme emerges, which is the importance of reconciling oneself with one's imperfections, and of finding comfort in ordinary everyday life. Cotton mentions coming from a 'working-class background' and her struggles with depression, while Emma Freud, who is married to the writer and film producer Richard Curtis, describes how they prefer evenings with friends to nights on the red carpet. Resilience comes into these narratives, now part of the common-sense of dealing with adversity. The magazine thus pitches itself some steps away from the assemblage of elements we have come to associate with the perfect, even as its interviewees are themselves not only in the spotlight of success but, in the case of Cotton, is married into a dynasty of rock star wealth. However, what they all profess is a need to acknowledge their failings and not feel they all are having to judge themselves against ideas of a perfect life. There is then an editorial convergence effect around this theme of pulling back from ideas of the perfect life; instead we must learn to love ourselves as we are. There is a triteness here, banal also in the way it is repeated across so many feminine genres, the new urgency coming from a perceived mental health crisis among young women. What can be seen here is the deployment of the *p-i-r* as an editorial strategy, so as not to deter the advertisers from the fashion and beauty industries. We might conjecture, in the absence of ethnographic accounts, that in this milieu of media professionals there is in place a supply-chain of accumulated insight into what readers and viewers and possible target markets are looking for in the purchases they make. Budgets will be apportioned to various research agencies often themselves employing young women graduates in arts, humanities and social sciences to investigate the new feminist landscape which can then be wrought in terms more compatible with a shareholder-friendly feminine consumer culture.

Critique of Resilience

How have scholars in the social sciences and in cultural studies approached the question of resilience? Two distinctive perspectives have emerged. One from Rose and Lentzos urges caution in the critique of resilience, as we will see below; the other is feminist and more attentive to popular culture, and it seeks to display connections between the cultural values of neoliberalism and resilience techniques (Rose and Lentzos 2016).[17] Nikolas Rose and Filippa Lentzos stage a provocative intervention. We might forgive their slightly querulous tone on the grounds of Rose's standing in the field, as among the first to work exhaustively with the Foucault writings on power and biopolitics and what Rose called 'advanced liberalism'. The claim here is that there is a tendency to sweepingly conflate this array of resilience practices with neoliberalism in a reductive way. This avoids 'the complexities of careful analysis and evaluation ...' '(N)eoliberalism [becomes] ... an all-purpose term of critique in much contemporary critical social science ...' leading to 'totalizing analyses' where neoliberalism is ubiquitous and omnipresent, a catch-all phrase and thus a sociological banality.

> Is neoliberalism an ideology, a doctrine, a political project, a strategy, an epoch? When the term is used, does it refer to "actually existing" neoliberalism – which takes complex and hybrid forms in different contexts – or is it an interpretive notion .... Or is it merely a term of critique applied to policies that seem to turn their backs on the major structural reforms necessary to overcome poverty and disadvantage, leaving these to the mercy of markets, competition and the search for private profit, while urging each individual to become an entrepreneur themselves, or be consigned to a twilight world of exclusion?
>
> (Rose and Lentzos 2016, p. 19)

From training regimes in elite schools for 'character', to notions of industriousness instilled into working-class children, responsibility and resilience have, over a much longer period than its current critics suggest, been integral across a wide range of social institutions from the military and security apparatuses to disaster planning. The authors also point out that leftist critiques of resilience as the preferred tool of neoliberalism, when welfare and social services provisions are being reduced and privatized, overlook the fierce critiques of the welfare state emanating from the left from the 1970s to the 1990s, when it was attacked for its bureaucracy, its ignoring of the grassroots and its mechanisms of social control. Rose and Lentzos then remind readers that resilience ideas as well as notions of citizenship were always part of the development of the welfare state (see also Riley 1992). It is not as though one bad set of principles has simply replaced a previously good set. These words of caution are for sure a useful corrective to a tendency, perhaps, for feminist cultural studies scholars to rush in and draw too hasty conclusions.[18] But feminist cultural studies are often driven by a sense of urgency and by a commitment to making a kind of diagnosis of our present conditions of living, as a template for more extended scholarship. Our studies are often pursued tentatively, in the hope of highlighting and making connections so as to draw attention to something that is taking place in the here and now. This kind of work conforms more with the model established by Stuart Hall, attempting a conjunctural analysis by drawing together seemingly dispersed elements and showing how ideological patterns converge by means of articulation effects, to produce a new politics of meaning. Rose and Lentzos pay close attention to some of the historical features of resilience training, but they do not consider its place within the popular media today. Nor do they engage with its particular gender dynamics or with its current prominence as a defining theme in consumer culture.

We can see then that the *p-i-r*, introduced and then firmly ensconced within the everyday ephemera of feminine pop culture, plays a role in translating from the new activist feminism to the embedded power relations which underscore contemporary capitalism and its consumer culture. *P-i-r* bridges the gap between feminism and capitalism, delivering something that is palatable and that will not deter advertisers. Gill and Orgad point out that resilience techniques addressed to women are also a response to the harsh economic conditions following the banking crisis of 2008 (Gill and Orgad 2018). Resilience is therefore associated with the way that austerity economics were presented to the public by government as the only viable pathway to avoid further recession. Women must therefore find feminine ways of dealing with stress and uncertainty, they must learn to adapt and accommodate.[19] The prevalence of apps for confidence training also marks out the contours of a privatized way of managing and overseeing the social effects of gender inequality. Gill and Orgad refer to the many adjurations to women to find ways of 'bouncing back' from difficulties in family life or in the workplace (Gill and Orgad 2018). The magazine they look at encourages readers to 'give up on being perfect', and instead to focus on learning to be resilient. Magazines like *Marie-Claire* suggest how readers can navigate their way through the climate of economic uncertainty with the help of confidence techniques and self-improvement workshops and seminars. If popular feminism has alerted women to the inequalities which accrue to their gender position and some of its consequences (imposter syndrome, etc.) then resilience techniques are at hand to play some role in addressing this disadvantage. Thus the 'psychological turn' is understood by Gill and Orgad as part of the way contemporary neoliberal society institutes norms of female selfhood that have recourse to resilience techniques, while disavowing ideas of political anger accruing from perceived gender injustice.

The argument presented here attributes to resilience a more ambivalent role: yes, it substitutes as an alternative to the collectivist and organizational energies required of a new feminist politics – and so it does indeed stand as a substitute for earlier, more caring regimes, essentially for welfare – but more specifically it draws audiences and readers back from the cliff edge of hard neoliberal leadership-feminism, towards the more familiar terrain of liberal feminism, where work–life balances signal, ironically, a less altered gendered hierarchy in the field of paid employment, especially in the corporate world. Resilience thus becomes a catch-all term, multi-functional and predicated on a logic of substitution, and thereby standing in for some things that have been lost to women as a result of welfare dismantling, while also nudging up against and displacing currently existing phenomena such as the new feminism, without entirely dismantling its field of influence, as if speculating on its terms of profitability and, if pushed, endorsing a variation of liberal feminism as a force for manageable changes to the gender regime. When the social world increasingly defines itself in terms of anxiety and uncertainty, and when it is seen as shameful to be dependent on others, the need for resilience also becomes part of our everyday common-sense, one which binds us to its terms and reconciles us to its conditions. This popular truth, as all truths do, has the ability to become a kind of inevitability, reducing our capacity to think or act otherwise. Because they are so widely in circulation, we find ourselves taking up these vocabularies and using them, even as we doubt them or refute them.

'The Violence of Regulatory Norms' (Butler 1997)

Thus far our critique of resilience revolves round its role as a pro-capitalist therapeutic device attending to, while nevertheless reproducing, the ills wrought upon women as a consequence of prevailing gender inequalities, and also deriving from the specific constellation of contemporary life as a time of risk, uncertainty and precarity. The *p-i-r* can also be understood as a replenishing factor, injecting into feminine consumer culture an element of innovation that derives from the new wave of feminist activism. The *p-i-r*, under these circumstances, and with its spread across popular culture, can assuage the more radical threat posed by new feminisms, usurp its place while also stealing some of its thunder. In this subterfuge role it seems to propose a pathway back to liberal feminism away from the excessive competitiveness of neoliberal leadership-feminism. But what would it mean, by way of a conclusion, to subject this configuration of cultural norms directed towards women to a more psychoanalytic consideration? Popular culture is by definition a place of simplification and easy-to-absorb messages. In its entertainment mode it seeks to arouse pleasure and enjoyment, it distracts from the serious problems of the day or else it offers pithy and reassuring advice. While we can hardly then criticize popular culture for failing to provide its readers or audiences with more complex understandings of gender and sexuality, or with more sophisticated aesthetics, we can perhaps provide more insight into the seeming appeal of the *p-i-r* and what keeps it as such a defining feature of feminine popular culture today. What is the basis of our attachment to self-beratement and to the genres which preserve and perpetuate this activity, even as they also seek to repair the damage done?

The psychoanalyst and author Adam Phillips, writing in the *London Review of Books* (5 March 2015) reflects on the pervasiveness of self-beratement in contemporary society. He reminds us that we are all ambivalent beings, which means that in relation to things or persons who are important to us, including ourselves, love and hatred are entwined and exist alongside each other. This is different from merely having 'mixed feelings' about someone or something. It is the important things that we are ambivalent about. 'Where there is self-hatred there is also self-love.' It is the Freudian super-ego which is the source of self-beratement: 'self criticism can be our most unpleasant – our most sadomasochistic ... way of loving ourselves' (Phillips 2015, p. 13). Like the various genres of feminine pop culture, the super-ego is characterized by its narrow repertoire, it is always saying the same thing, coming back to us with the same accusations, it is like a 'stuck record', 'boring and cruel' – it reproaches us with the same old failings and in so doing relentlessly conveys a wider sense of dissatisfaction. But we like this process of self-recrimination, it appeals to us, and this perhaps accounts for our attachment to (self-help) genres of media which seem to specialize in activating, in an appetising way, this corner of psychic life. Phillips reminds us that earlier concepts of conscience in Freud's writing later transform into the super-ego, whereby our anger and desire for vengeance is turned against ourselves as a reproach for harbouring murderous thoughts: 'we murder ourselves through self reproach ... we mutilate our own character ... with an unrelenting violence ... we prejudge ourselves in a way that obscures rather than advances self knowledge' (Phillips 2015, p. 14). All the more so perhaps for women, who historically have been typecast as less aggressive than their male counterparts, domestic peace-makers and 'angels of the house'. The super-ego also makes us fearful that 'we can even lose our minds'; it is way too powerful and it makes us solipsistic and less capable of social exchange, we are ever more isolated and more solitary. Phillips then asks, 'why are we then so bewitched by our own self hatred?' (Phillips 2015, p. 15).

Bearing this in mind, we could, at this point, interject, and consider how the *p-i-r* has established itself as a horizon of cultural intelligibility for women. Its ubiquitous presence across so many media and social media locations means that it becomes a dominant frame of reference for understanding female complaint. We could surmise that it slips unobtrusively into the space of the super-ego and in so doing activates and articulates the link between the social and the psychic. Phillips sees the super-ego working like a spell, it has a hypnotic effect. It becomes dogma. It bullies us. We go along with it, fearful of its power and its apparent claim to know who we really are. Its intimate voice (again something mimicked in the women's magazine format) claims to know us so well. 'Self criticism is an unforbidden pleasure: we seem to relish the way it makes us suffer' (Phillips 2015, p. 14). Hence our ambivalence: we are hooked into these intimate murmurings even as we wish to be free of them, even as we dispute what Phillips calls the 'standards' they impose upon us. The appeal of the *p-i-r* is that it is able to speak in this private intimate voice. This has always been the special effect of the women's magazine genre. So when a 17-year-old girl says to herself, 'I make a promise to myself this year to work so hard in school and to gain all the A Levels I need to get into a top university, and make my parents proud, and I will also go out for a run every morning before school so that I do not put on weight, and I will also learn how to be resilient so that when I get racially abused at school because of being mixed race and because I am more ambitious than my classmates I will be able to deal with it and not let it hurt me' – when she says this, we could argue that she has taken heed of the advice she has found when reading magazines and popular literature, and that this has been encrypted into the super-ego which will tick her off when she finds it hard to keep the promise to herself and is troubled by the idea that she has let herself down.

Phillips provides us with a useful way of thinking about the *p-i-r* in psychoanalytic terms and, though he does not focus on gender, there is scope to make this move, for the reason that, like Butler in her various recent writings, Phillips refers to the influence of cultural norms as well as the socio-historical environment on how the psyche is formed. This

allows us to think about our current times, where individualization and 'self responsibility' are so highly valued, and
where it is shameful to be dependent. And when Phillips talks
about self-beratement and asks why we are so bewitched
by our self-hatred, feminists will quickly point out that it is
young women who are so prone to self-hatred. And when it
comes to talking about fostering the unforbidden pleasures
of self-criticism, it is easy to see how popular culture makes
itself available for undertaking this task, precisely because
it seems to tell us the reasons for our discontent and the
means to overcome it. And then we must also remind
ourselves of the gender asymmetry at the heart of consumer
culture, with the genre of the women's magazine historically
constituting a form for which there is no male equivalent.
It therefore stands as an unparalleled and privileged space
for the production of femininity. Phillips considers the
super-ego as a source of spiteful dogma, paternal authority,
and of course of harsh judgement; it does not take much
sociological effort to surmise that this psychic force finds
fertile ground in the beauty-fashion complex, in advertising
and in those spaces of consumer culture which have historically given themselves over to the 'making up' of normative
womanhood. The make-up of the super-ego depends, then,
on the culture around us, on prevailing popular moralities.
Phillips describes how it intimidates us into complicity; all
the more so because it seems to know us well, and because
'self criticism is an unforbidden pleasure'.[20] All of which
means that while we will feel ourselves to be failing (not good
enough, not perfect enough, not losing weight fast enough),
we lose a capacity to reflect on where all of these 'standards',
as Phillips labels them, are coming from; we seem less able to
inquire as to how these expectations and requirements come
into being. Our critical voices are stifled. This is just what we
have come to expect.

Psychoanalytic practice seems to be uniquely able to prise
apart and interrupt the flow of the super-ego's address to
the compliant self. It does so, according to Phillips, by being
able to offer a multiplicity of other perspectives, other ways
of understanding the self, which of course is the job of the
analyst in her encounters with the patient. We only cling
onto this horizon of power inscribed within our own inner

mental landscape, claims Phillips, because it offers a kind of security. It is plausible because it is so tedious, so endlessly boring. Phillips seems to suggest through his references throughout the essay to Hamlet and Don Quixote (both favourites of Freud) that, alongside psychoanalysis, great literature can also be a force of interruption, breaking the stranglehold of the super-ego. We might say then that, except on a few occasions, the job of popular culture is to feed off a repertoire of familiar and accommodating vocabularies, introducing a twist here and there, making some changes in line with what is going on in the social world so as to appear current.[21] If, however, we are looking for the kind of complexity that Adam Phillips seeks as a way of both under-standing and dislodging this loud voice of admonishment, while also contesting the very notion of a coherent, self-standing and self-sufficient subjectivity, then we must turn to art and literature, or to psychoanalytic practice, rather than to the quick fixes of positivistic psychology translated into so many self-help genres. But does this not inevitably favour middle-class and well-educated young women? This leaves the less privileged exposed only to the resilience tips of pop culture, from Beyoncé or Lady Gaga.[22] While Adam Phillips' essay certainly gives rise to any number of questions as to the interruptive and complexifying power of art, literature and clinical practice as against the banalities of the *p-i-r*, it is valuable not only for bringing psychoanalysis back into the picture, but also because it challenges to the core the common-sense appeal of the *p-i-r*, its endorsement among other things of a simplified and unified sense of self, and the way it encourages adjustment to and accommodation with a status quo.

Conclusions

In the early 2000s some of these same concerns were within my own sociological orbit, where the high visibility of female disorders, especially body-image related illnesses, were so prominent in a context where unlike our current time there was a widescale repudiation of both feminism

and LGBTQ politics. I explored this terrain as female melancholia, drawing on Butler's psychoanalytic concerns with
heterosexual melancholia and also with rage. I designated
the wide range of bodily anxieties as post-feminist disorders,
on the basis that there was knowledge on the part of young
women that their 'plaints' connected in some way or another
with the injustices of the gender regime. I thus argued that
the young women were gender aware, but that they were
in denial or had repressed this knowledge for the sake of
feminine cultural intelligibility as girls, in a context where
feminism was repudiated and even considered distasteful
and repugnant. Budgeon also suggested that eating disorders
had become so normalized as to be considered simply part
of what it is to be a woman, thus fostering everyday forms
of solidarity formed around this seeming reality without
this precipitating any necessary feminist identity (Budgeon
2003). This normalization of feminine pathology permitted
a deciphering of this culture of self-harm as a 'refracted
indictment of social norms' (Butler 1997). There was an
evisceration of feminism with no sign of a renewed sexual
politics springing into being. Feminism, as a haunting force,
which may have lingered somewhere in historical memory,
had to be cast aside. I argued then that in being required to
give up this feminism that they knew about, even loved, it
was preserved melancholically in the lives of its subjects as
somehow nameless and unavowed. From Freud to Bhabha,
Butler understood melancholia and its illegible rages as
emerging from lost ideals, such as a country, or cause, such as
liberty or freedom (se also Eng and Han 2000). Melancholia
marked the space of a 'rebellion put down', with the consequence that there might be a 'recasting of social plaint as
psychic self-judgement'. But is it not the case today that we
now enter a new terrain, where feminism is not just avowed
but a ubiquitous force in everyday life?

   In addition we have witnessed the full force of various
forms of anger and rage at gender injustice and sexual
inequality. So, through the hard work and frenetic activity of
online campaigning, organization, demonstrations, manifesto
writing, public declarations, media productions, a new form
of feminism is born, dating more or less from 2008 onwards.
The key question then is how to gauge the challenge to the

socio-economic field, indeed to capitalism, posed by the new feminism? And how to make sense of the spiralling rates of mental ill health and eating disorders and so on, now that there is no longer such disapprobation for feminist activity, now that young women can publicly express their rage at sexual and other injustices? That which haunted the edges of consciousness is now more fully reinstated in everyday life, the melancholic source has been named, avowed and thus expelled from its lonely place. How to decipher this situation, where a lost idea finds itself reinstated and when the melancholia of that time is seemingly extinguished? How do we tally the plethora of much more visible and marked out maladies of depression and anxiety which, in the time between the moment of 'post-feminist' melancholia and the current times of feminist activism, have found themselves centre-stage? These exist within a media luminosity of attention, pathologies which must be both addressed and treated, not with the vocabulary of psychoanalysis, but rather with the techniques of behavioural psychology such as CBT. Feminism, it seems, is no longer a lost cause, it has become an 'appearance'. This gives rise to many sociological questions, as well as questions of the psyche, that remain to be answered. For example, how do girls at school, hitherto uninterested in or suspicious of sexual politics, come to feminism? What is the nature of these encounters? How do they take up this mantle of feminism, stating loudly that they are 'feminists'? In the face of such big questions as these, the focus of attention in this current chapter has been a modest attempt to dissect the work of the *p-i-r*, which attempts to reconcile a seemingly feminist-femininity with consumer culture and with capitalism in general (Banet-Weiser 2018).

But there is a good deal more to the *p-i-r* than simply being an instrument for blandifying and sanitizing feminist critique so as to maintain the status quo and the profit margins of the fashion-beauty complex. It also has a moral purpose. And here we can turn yet again to Butler (2004). In *Giving an Account of Oneself* Butler is setting her position up against a number of ongoing issues in political culture. She considers the various calls to popular morality that have come into play in recent years, often having to do with the importance of taking responsibility for the self, and not being dependent.

Butler reminds readers that Adorno, writing in the context of 1930s Germany, understood popular moralities as 'ethical violence', and we could extend this to nowadays, to suggest that underpinning the *p-i-r* is a violent intent. The popular morality of resilience-training as an aspect of the gender regime, the emphasis on not being dependent on others, or on the state, takes the form of a kind of call to duty, articulating a new definition of female citizenship with all of the attendant exclusions that this implies. The dire logic here is that all women are set up to fail, but some more dramatically unequally than others, so that overall, the status quo of the gender regime is upheld. At best this incurs a climate of constant and remorseless social disapproval and negative self-judgement, even as one is inveighed upon to reconcile oneself with and make good of one's imperfections. Not only is one locked within the cage of the sovereign self, self-berating as Adam Phillips describes, but for those who are, for reasons of poverty and racial disadvantage, removed from or excluded by the direct remit of the *p-i-r*, its indirect address, cloaked in the language of resilience for austerity, provides even more reasons to self-castigate, for making bad choices in sexual partners, for lacking self-esteem, having children too young, for not getting good enough qualifications – in effect a litany of self-blame factors (Gill and Orgad 2018). In this scenario the *p-i-r* amplifies the very conditions it purportedly seeks to resolve, this is its pharmakon effect.

Butler (echoing the commentary by Adam Phillips referred to above) has long contested the idea of a unified, autonomous and transparent self as well as the perils in pursuing this as a psychic ideal. She has gone to great lengths to challenge this sovereign notion of the individual in possession of mastery. There is an ideal of self-mastery and self-responsibility as something that could be accomplished by undertaking the right kinds of prescribed actions. Against this Butler has consistently argued that a more just society would comprise persons who might avow our interdependence and the need to provide care and shelter and to show compassion. Butler finds in the writing of Cavavero, Laplanche and Levinas a series of arguments about our relationality and about how an ethics can emerge from our failure of self-transparency, and how such an ethics can also work against violence, as a force for reduction of violence. Cavavero envisages a more relational politics by asking, who are you? We turn to a you. This is also to say that '*I am my relation to you*' (Butler 2005, p. 81). Here we have a social theory based on the 'who?' Here we see a possible generosity: the other, the who who makes a claim on me, and to whom I turn, because they are also me. It is then our relationality which promises an ethics of anti-violence, a means of disconnecting from the violence against the self which is only reproduced by the *p-i-r*. The pop culture prism of the *p-i-r* which has been the subject of this current investigation seeks to instate a norm of selfhood, prone to endless self-beratement, repudiating our deeper obligations and responsibilities to the other, while purporting to embody a popular morality the extent of which might be the offering of oneself as a role model or mentor to younger women, that they might follow in our more successful footsteps. This is also the logic of the meritocracy (Littler 2017).

To conclude, this chapter has queried the place of a certain mechanism or device, one that circulates through the field of the feminine popular media and which has been labelled the *p-i-r* for the work it does in managing the presence of new forms of feminism and its many activisms, especially as these become available for young women as they are exposed to the disciplinary apparatuses of consumer culture as well as the gendering norms manifest in family life and in education. The *p-i-r* can then be seen as a capitalist way of profiting from feminism, while intervening in and interfering with its multiple practices and its presence as an appearance. The work of resilience-training is, as James has pointed out, all-consuming, leaving the new feminine subject at the mercy of an unsustainable ideal of selfhood (James 2015). While the *p-i-r* pervades our everyday common-sense as a kind of feminist-inflected popular morality, it also heralds an extension of past powerful notions of feminine virtue (the angel in the house) and a reproduction of the exclusions of feminine-maternal citizenship as they too were inscribed within traditional genres, such as women's magazines and other popular formats (Riley 1992). The ethical violence here was not only predicated on the 'cruel optimism' invoked but also on the privatized shaming of those who might read the pages or view the pictures, only to be silenced by the exclusively white terms of the address. With Berlant, we might agree that these forms of mass culture have succeeded in their longevity by tapping into psychic pleasures of femininity to exact cruel outcomes such as the dream of the good life. With Butler, we might argue that this cruelty transforms into everyday rituals of ethical violence, a meritocratic micropolitics predicated on commercially sponsored resilient feminist-inclined female subjects for whom selfhood implies a seemingly achievable strength which abjures relationality, weakness and dependency.

3
Out of Welfare: Women and 'Contraceptive Employment'

> As I think it was Roepke said, what is an unemployed person?
> He is not someone suffering from an economic disability: he is
> not a social victim. He is a worker in transit. He is a worker in
> transit between an unprofitable activity and a more profitable
> activity. (Foucault 2006, p. 139)

> ... How is ... social policy conceptualized in a welfare
> economy? ... a social policy in a welfare economy is
> acceptance of the principle that stronger growth should entail
> a more active, intense (and) generous social policy as a kind of
> reward and compensation. (Foucault 2006, p. 142)

We have so far indicated the multi-functional and important
status of the term resilience. Firstly we have seen it playing
a mediating role as part of the *p-i-r* between new articulations of feminism as they develop a capacity to challenge the
feminine genres of consumer culture and thus of capitalism
itself; secondly we have seen it stand in for feminism as a
technique for individualized 'technologies of the self', for
female empowerment (Banet-Weiser 2018); thirdly we have
shown it to be a boundary-marking activity that serves to
harden divisions of class as well as race and ethnicity among
young women, thus diminishing the capacity for feminist unity
and solidarity; and fourthly we have identified how it plays a
role in smoothing a pathway away from ideas of the welfare
state towards notions of therapeutic self-responsibilization,

which in turn invokes ideas of self-esteem that penalize the poor and disadvantaged, and in our case poor women, by labelling them as lacking the self-confidence to find a job or career, and thus as being somehow responsible for their own predicament.[1] This last is in spite of the fact that in reality there are so many structural factors, such as inadequate educational opportunities in areas of high unemployment as well as embedded patterns of poverty in rundown regions, which lock so many people into cycles of unemployment or the possibility only of intermittent, low-paid and casual work. The way in which these issues are talked about forms a new kind of popular morality addressing audiences, readers and viewers in particularly intensive ways.

In this chapter I begin to consider what we might describe as a part of the neoliberal destiny for those women in the UK who are not among that section of the female population that can easily take part in the various requirements to 'enhance their human capital' (Brown 2015). These are women for whom the addresses of the *p-i-r* (as referred to in the previous chapter) are at best exclusionary, at worst aggressive and offensive. That is, low-qualified, unskilled disadvantaged women, including single mothers, black and ethnic minority women who are materially disadvantaged, women with care obligations, poor migrant women, those living in areas of high unemployment, in post-industrial parts of the country, disabled women as well as women who are part of the lower echelons of the working class, who are pushed towards workfare, and finally simply women and especially mothers who are in precarious relationships with unsupportive partners. Considering this population from the viewpoint of a feminist cultural studies approach, I begin with some brief observations about the fate of the welfare state as understood by feminist political theorists, notably Wendy Brown. From here I propose an argument about how work, even low-paid and casual work, is proffered to such women as, among other things, a way of restoring the damage to femininity wrought by 'dependency'. Morality is feminized to emphasize self-esteem, respectability and pride in personal appearance and so on. In this guise popular morality echoes with Foucault's emphasis on the body and on the 'conduct of conduct' (Foucault 2006). I foreground

popular culture and media as being tasked with carrying this
out as a kind of civic duty. For women to become eligible to
the calls of the *p-i-r* they must achieve the bottom-line status
of being in work. We might envisage overall the transition
'out of welfare' as a matter of the Job Centres somehow
acting in conjunction with those various forms of media and
popular culture, including Reality TV, so as to rescue failing
femininities, bringing them into a realm where the post-
welfare discourses can do their work.[2]

Wendy Brown's reading of Foucault's lectures on biopolitics points to how much emphasis neoliberal economists,
including the German Ordoliberals of the 1920s and 1930s,
placed on a range of principles: on the reduction of welfare;
making the 'old forms of social protection illegible'; delegiti-
mating the state's role in wealth redistribution; revoking
entirely the idea that welfare is somehow 'compensatory
for capitalism's ill effects'; and intensifying inequality for
the sake of competition (Brown 2015; Foucault 2006).
Brown refers to the 'economization of social policy' and
she also alludes to the fact that refamilialization is key to
this process. If the welfare state is 'hollowed out', becoming
almost 'unrecognizable', then what fills that space? 'New
arrangements and practices' have to be developed (ibid., p.
63). One clear answer in the UK in the period starting in the
1980s is that, no longer in a counter-posing relationship with
capitalism, but instead moving swiftly to a more harmonious
partnership, the state looks to the private sector. Emanating
from the world-leading business schools, the 'New Public
Management' provides the appropriate vocabulary. The
welfare state is increasingly absolved of its social care responsibilities and instead gradually redefines itself as the purveyor
of a new moral economy of work and workfare. In the pages
that follow, I develop a three-pronged argument: *first* that
work and workfare for women are favoured means by which
neoliberalism adopts or co-opts something of a feminist
rhetoric ('neoliberal feminism');[3] *second* that popular culture
and the popular media, making use of various entertainment
formats, step forward to act as agents for welfare reform;
and *third* that in the UK work is foregrounded as the means
by which the family is enabled to shoulder the burden of the
social goods once provided by the state. Unlike in the US

(as we will consider in the pages that follow), work is the preferred route to 'responsibilization', meaning that disadvantaged mothers must prioritize paid labour.

One of the overwhelming realities of women's experience, and of young women's pathways within the frame of current socio-economic arrangements, is the prospect of a full working life. Within the patriarchal terms which still obtain, those who are deemed highly employable subjects are constantly prevailed upon to be thankful, as if this status were both a gift, something granted us, and a mark of social progress. If, as Brown argues, neoliberal rationality operates by means of a disembowelling of democracy, leaving a hollowed-out space of de-politicization (close to what I also proposed in *The Aftermath of Feminism*), then nowadays, with the recent upsurge of feminist campaigning, the potency of work as an individualistic alternative to everything that is involved in the adoption of a feminist politics, is all the more palpable (Brown 2015; McRobbie 2008). That is, work and career become goals *instead of* struggles for changes to work and for gender equality. We could label this the preferred pathway for a pragmatic right-wing feminism today. Employment for women becomes a defining mark of status and identity. This centrality of the working woman also extends into and indeed is magnified many times over within those gender and development discourses which are integral to the neoliberal values adopted by organizations such as the World Bank, as well as by so many aid agencies (Wilson 2015). As Kalpana Wilson shows in detail, there is a direct appeal to women as being implicitly more reliable and more moral subjects than their male counterparts, and thus worthy of investment (Wilson 2015). This is manifest in the *Gender Economics as Smart Economics* programmes which focus on the 'hyper-industrious and entrepreneurial girl' (ibid., p. 809). The history of these recent programmes from the early 1990s, including the 2004 *Nike Girl Effect* projects and several others since, all point to this foregrounding of work. Kalpana Wilson credits this racializing adoption of 'the girl' with an 'infinite capacity for labour' as de-politicizing on many counts (ibid., p. 818). Far from promoting gender equality, it diminishes such a possibility through a lack of attention to structural inequalities in favour of individual endeavour narratives.

My concern in this chapter is primarily with the UK, and the requirement that women work in contemporary British society, as well as the chastisement meted out to those who appear to evade such expectations. I also aim to develop a better understanding of contemporary anti-welfarism, as a distinctive trope of neoliberal reason, and how the abjection of what is presented as the unrespectable or unkempt body of the working-class woman plays a role in this process. While there is a whole library of cruel nineteenth-century depictions of the 'slum-dwelling' working-class woman, this recent abjection-effect demonstrates the centrality of conduct within neoliberal rationality, and it highlights what failure to present oneself in such a way as to enhance one's human capital looks like (Brown 2015). If, as Brown reminds us, anti-welfarism is a defining feature of the repertoire of neoliberal core values, then women, as a category of persons for whom the post-war welfare apparatus has been a key source of support (as well as disciplining), are disproportionately affected by the drive to reduce welfare across all of its current institutions and functions.[4] Feminists in the past have argued that the welfare apparatus is primarily concerned with women and children, despite its insurance elements being predicated historically on the male breadwinner. At the same time this had the consequence of putting black and migrant women at further disadvantage, not just because of the more intense surveillance and disciplining they have experienced, but also for the reason that their husbands have been excluded from mainstream labour markets (Wilson 1975; Shilliam 2018).

So the question then is how have women recently come to be configured in this dismantling of welfare? One answer to this question is that working-class women are now fully defined as workers. In terms of contemporary biopolitics, this means that they are a female population who will not be dependent on the state. Or rather one for whom any remaining benefits will be paid to them on the basis that they are already in employment, and even then only with conditions. The focus in the UK on economic activity as a social good for all women of working age means that family obligations are pushed, for better or worse, into a secondary place, with the exception of that small strata of well-off women who can make the 'choice' to prioritize home-making. Even then there is a deficit of status when children grow up, leaving the stay-at-home mother in need of an activity which brings rank and recognition. Overall fertility in the UK is defined within the normative frame of planned parenthood. This is a complex terrain where social policy and public health both work seemingly by stealth or behind the scenes to reshape family life so that it accords with the requirements of the new economy. It is hard to find government policy documents explicitly stating this seeming downgrading of family in favour of work.[5] Instead it is within the media and celebrity-driven popular culture that these encouragements take place, where specifically middle-class and white norms of successful femininity require the putting off of having children until 'the time is right'.

With the proviso that women first get ahead with a career or at least a regular job, family life is being made to comply more emphatically with the nuclear model. It is being 'responsibilized', an awkward term, as Brown points out, but one which indicates the web of calculations required for 'family planning'. As the welfare state aims to shed its role in supporting social reproduction, so must the family show itself to be up for this task. Responsibility for this rests, at least partly, on the working two-parent unit. No one is more openly disparaged than the single mother, especially if she has more than one child. She exemplifies the current idea of a 'social problem', and for the historic reasons of slavery and the post-slave experience, which shattered the possibilities for stable nuclear family arrangements, this exposes many black British women to multiple levels of discrimination. The UK differs here from the US, as Melinda Cooper has shown: the power of US Christian values means that there is, and has been, a more punitive anti-feminist ethos in place, with feminism being blamed for encouraging women out to work, making them more independent and less tied to men (Cooper 2017). Feminism is thus charged with playing a role in the break-up of the family. Ideally women should be dependent on a male breadwinner, and when this is not a viable option workfare is doubly tainted with the mark of female failure. It is against this backdrop that someone like Ivanka Trump can cast herself as a modernizing feminist, defending mothers who want to work (Trump 2017; Rottenberg 2018).

In the UK, regular work encourages what we might call a contraceptive-effect.[6] Further or higher education with the prospect of a job and income has the effect of delaying motherhood. Easily available access to birth control is offered to working-class and low-qualified young women (as well as to their middle-class counterparts) in the hope that they do not become single mothers. The further twist in this *dispositif* of 'contraceptive-employment' is that it avoids a directly racializing slur with regard to Afro-Caribbean families which, for reasons referred to above, have not conformed to the ideal of the white European nuclear family.[7] By these same measures, however, a further social polarization effect occurs, marking off those economically disadvantaged women who have children within what are dubbed irregular relationships, from those on the other side. The Facebook world of happy nuclear families with their regular postings in the Mumsnet mode can only further intensify the feelings of inadequacy or failure for those women who have children but no partner to pose alongside them. Work, and in this case low-paid and typically insecure labour, is a primary space of control for disadvantaged women.[8] The workfare system is intimately connected to changes to welfare. The decimation of benefits also goes hand-in-hand with changes in the world of work. Women, including single mothers, are being drafted into work, often with the threat of losing benefits if they refuse or if they turn down available jobs, even if these are on 'zero hours' contracts. The imperative to work brings into play a large number of agencies: those who assess the health of the claimant and his or her ability to work, those who match clients to employers and those who train job-seekers. As Lisa Adkins has pointed out, contemporary workfare inaugurates a welter of legal procedures, 'socio-technical devices', training manuals, as well as new offices and agencies (Adkins 2016). In effect a market is brought into being, 'a market for the labour of the unemployed' (ibid.). Service providers tender for valuable contracts to place job-seekers in companies signed up to the workfare programmes.

Once again a different strategy is pursued in the US, where the (extended) family must now function as the substitute for welfarism (Cooper 2017). The reason why it has proved possible to force the family in a low-wage economy to shoulder almost the entire burden of social reproduction, is that the two prevailing political forces of the right, the neoconservatives and the neoliberals, find common ground in pinpointing family and kinship as the altruistically driven locus for providing members of society with social security and protection.[9] Social neoconservatives argue that feminism and the various progressive movements such as *War on Poverty* undermined the family. With welfare in their pockets, the unemployed were freed from their obligations to each other. The costs to the nation for welfare spiralled as women – in the conventional stereotype African-American women – chose to bring up children alone without a male breadwinner. (This pathologization of the black family, Cooper reminds us, also usefully took attention away from endemic structural and institutional racism and segregation.) The point for the US neoliberals is to resecure these ties of family and kinship as a replacement for welfare, even if this seems like an unlikely prospect and in fact escalates destitution. Cooper notes the ways in which poor families become mired in debt.[10] Having access to high-interest credit for many of those needs which might otherwise be provided for by the state, i.e. 'asset-based welfare', means that family members are also increasingly tied to each other and liable for each other's borrowing, such that the indebted poor family becomes its own container unit, from which it is difficult to escape. In the US family, indebtedness is all the more marked because welfare is so eviscerated, and the Christian-led emphasis on the family so entrenched.

Thanks to Keynesian post-war planning, public assistance has had a less stigmatized existence in the UK than in the US. Indeed, as Elizabeth Wilson argued back in 1975, those years of British history could be defined in terms of a widely adhered to 'ideology of the welfare state' (Wilson 1975). Christian right-wing conservatives, including the anti-abortion lobbies, have been much less vocal in the UK.[11] Nor is there any strong political force which unambiguously advocates that women's place is in the home.[12] New Labour, during its years in office from 1997 to 2007, adopted a secular stance, quietly championing free, safe birth control for young women on demand, which in turn played some role in its post-feminist ethos of choice and empowerment. In a sense it was this, along with its much-vaunted commitment to meritocracy, that permitted New Labour to regard itself as modern and forward-looking. Work has a preferential value, something spearheaded through the years of the New Labour government under Tony Blair and when Gordon Brown was first Chancellor and then for a short time Prime Minister. Being in work now ensures avoidance of the stigma of being work-shy, or of being a 'skiver' rather than a 'striver', as the former Chancellor George Osborne put it.[13] Work, then, in the context of the specifically UK alignment of neoliberal values, takes precedence over a reliance on family values, while at the same time acquiring some degree of feminist credentials as progressive public policy, by being seen to grant women the possibility of economic independence. Thus, the single mother, if she is also in paid employment, redeems herself somewhat from an otherwise denigrated status.[14]

As Stuart Hall and Alan O'Shea note, it is the 'common-sense of neoliberalism' which acts as a forcefield for generating approval for these transformations of welfare (Hall and O'Shea 2013). This common-sense is formulated on the pages of the tabloid press, and in Reality TV series, which utilize various techniques aimed at shaming people on benefits. We might call this the 'imaginary of anti-welfarism'. To sum up, one key element of the transition in British society to a fully neoliberal regime is that disadvantaged women are compelled to prioritize paid labour and 'contraceptive employment' (often at the low-pay end) over and above maternal obligations or indeed the desire to become a mother.[15] Participation in work signals respectability for that section of the female population for whom such a self-definition is essential yet also frequently denied. State-sponsored as well as commercially endorsed femininity has, for more than a century, defined and advocated white middle-class norms of appearance and disposition, conduct and outlook. Failure to adhere to such values as these and the respectable status they imply, is in effect failure to succeed in being female, hence Skeggs's account of white working-class women's anxieties and hence also the significance of the idea of respectability in the everyday lives of black women (Skeggs 1997; Higginbotham 1994). With one's sexuality and identity at stake, the work ethic for women nowadays constitutes a new moral economy: being on benefits suggests a great deal more than economic hardship, it also means failed femininity and an abiding sense of shame. The old moral guardians have been replaced by various modes of attention, dispersed luminosities, seemingly random expressions of disgust, disapproval, disparaging words and phrases, abject images, clicks on like or dislike buttons, what Deleuze anticipated as 'control of communications' (Deleuze 1996). Despite the seemingly disorganized nature of these flows of moral disapprobation, my own preference for understanding this modality of power is to use the term visual media governmentality, for the reason that this points us back to older forms of consolidated state control and to media institutions that are now in states of transition and transformation – indeed of metamorphosis (Beck 2013).

'Sleeping off a Life on Benefits'[16]

I now consider how two influential Marxists, David Harvey and Wolfgang Streeck, have shown themselves to be unreceptive to feminist arguments about family, work and welfare in the context of contemporary neoliberalism (Harvey 2005; Streeck 2016). I then look to Stuart Hall as the cultural and political theorist whose writing proves more helpful in this respect. David Harvey is, of course, one of the best-known Marxist commentators on the rise of neoliberalism. He points to the shoring up of power in the business world, the decimation of trade union membership, the support for growth of jobs in non-union sectors, the demise of municipal socialism and, perhaps most saliently, wage stagnation alongside 'cuts in the social wage', all of which lead to the restoring of 'class power at the expense of labour' (Harvey 2005). Important as this contribution is, the key problems with Harvey's economistic account relate to his failure to consider the gender issues inscribed within the social wage. He gives scant attention to the media and cultural worlds, which have been spaces of intense activity in securing the consent of the population and of working-class people to the regime of anti-welfarism; and alongside this he embraces a theory of class power that does not take into account the critical importance of race, ethnicity and gender in modern civic society. Finally he ignores those cultural and ideological processes of individualization that have played a key role in breaking down traditional affiliations of class.[17] In this respect we can point to the enduring value of Ulrich Beck's and Elisabeth Beck-Gernscheim's writing on individualization (Beck and Beck-Gernscheim 2002).

Harvey uses the term social wage to refer to welfare and public services. In the past it was common to find the term family wage used instead, where it typically implied the male breadwinner model, assuming a wife at home. In 1975 Elizabeth Wilson noted Barbara Castle's oft-quoted definition of the family wage as a wage level based on available entitlements of the welfare state, from schools and hospitals to libraries and nurseries (Wilson 1975). Welfare provision then came to exist within a packaging of non-monetary social goods such as access to health and education and unemployment benefit, which were an integral part of the wage bargaining structure of industrial relations at a time when many sectors were still in the hands of the state. These benefits were presented as *de facto* part of the weekly wage, and they could be used by government as a way of holding down wages. This arrangement was also a key part of the so-called social contract: the idea that government was supporting industry by providing social goods and services (including free education and training, also subsidized council housing), which meant that the (primarily white and male) workforce would not make excessive wage demands to cover the costs of these provisions. Where Harvey is right to lament the loss of the social wage, he is less attentive to its role historically in supplementing the wages of that sector of the skilled male working class, typically the labour aristocracy. As Shilliam has persuasively reminded us, this was a racializing strategy that, in times of Windrush migration to Britain and its aftermath right up to the times of Enoch Powell in 1968, privileged a sector of the white working class, lifting them (and their families) upwards towards more highly skilled status while also inaugurating what Stuart Hall and others referred to as the 'age of affluence'. At the same time the existence of the social/family wage maintained and reinforced the existing sexual division of labour for white working-class British families.

Wolfgang Streeck, in his recent volume, adopts a fiercely anti-feminist stance, arguing that the entrance of middle-class women into the workplace in the last decades has thrown working-class men out of work, thus depriving working-class women of a breadwinner (Streeck 2016). He claims that 'worker militancy was vanquished ... by the mass entry of women into paid employment' (Streeck 2016, p. 98). Streeck bewails the losses wrought by neoliberalism to the families of the labour aristocracy. Capitalism eventually responds to rising unemployment by instituting flexible jobs, but for Streeck these jobs for women can only be construed as an assault on old labour. According to Streeck, the erosion by governments of the post-war welfare social contracts, which had been put in place with the aim of keeping organized labour and employers and big business happy, has produced deteriorated employment opportunities defined by flexibility and insecurity, low wages and de-unionization. This means that (assuming the heterosexual family unit) wives as well as their husbands are forced into more insecure work. Streeck understands contemporary capitalism as putting in place 'market conforming democracy'. Governments could no longer withstand the costs of the family wage, but neither could they tax big business; instead they borrowed until such a point that they could find ways of getting individuals to borrow themselves. Meanwhile the upward redistribution effect of low wages meant that global capitalism had plenty of money to lend, and thus capitalists lent first to governments and then increasingly to citizens and to the population at large, finally triggering the sub-prime crisis in 2008.

No matter how accurate this may be, Streeck comes across as a sourly anti-feminist man of labour and the trade unions in the old sense. For him, only the betrayed white working-class 'hausfrau' matters; there is no reference to disadvantaged or migrant or LGBTQ women, and middle-class women are simply job grabbers. There is no suggestion that gender inequality is an important thing to struggle against. Streeck goes so far as to take the imagined side of the working-class housewife whose stay-at-home status now marks out a 'personal disgrace' (Streeck 2016, p. 217). She is not just forced out to work, she has to work more hours to make up for the wage stagnation that has become so embedded in the modern work society. Streeck sees women in the workforce as being inherently passive, willing to work in non-unionized sectors, and 'happy to be employed at all', thus seriously undercutting male wages.[18] Women are now, he claims, less able to look after their children. They are no longer good housewives. With sarcasm, he refers to men being turned into 'new fathers'. This critique by Streeck, who is much admired within the left, demonstrates exactly the scale of the problem when we approach the question of women, work and welfare within the context of the neoliberal regime. Writing as a feminist and socialist, it becomes urgent for me both to make the case *for* and *against* work. Against, because this is the *sine qua non* of political freedom for women; and for, to fend off Streeck's misplaced left-wing nostalgia for a (short-lived) more protected era when (only) the white, working-class married woman could rely on her male breadwinner husband whose salary, along with the social wage, meant that she could fully attend to her role as home-maker.[19] The more significant question is the fate of the social wage in a context where, at least in the UK today, more than 70 per cent of mothers are active in the labour market, where real wages have indeed stagnated for so long, and where welfare is reduced and a range of benefits withdrawn. How does this decimation of public goods and services impact on women?

Stuart Hall, writing in the years of illness prior to his death in 2014, considers the emergence of neoliberalism within a frame of neo-Marxist cultural studies (Hall 2003, 2011). He pays close attention to the micro-politics of language and its potency when deployed in resonant ways across the media and in popular culture. This emphasis on language also allows Hall to reflect on everyday life and 'ordinary folk' and on how they are constantly addressed through these popular channels as part of an attempt to win them over to changes in the field of welfare. Hall and co-author Alan O'Shea use Gramsci extensively to interrogate the way in which the tabloid press has endorsed many policies emanating from government, while also laying the groundwork for the swift passage of new ones (Hall and O'Shea 2013). They note that from Thatcher through the Blair years the word *fairness* is used repeatedly. And likewise during the Coalition government of Cameron and Clegg, and in the context of an austerity budget, the then Chancellor George Osborne uses particularly vivid language to describe the workshy man or woman as 'sleeping off a life on benefits', unlike their neighbours who are willing to take a job even when their take-home pay falls beneath what some families get on benefits. The scene is thus set for benefits to be depicted as 'unfair'. For Gramsci, common-sense is 'episodic and disjointed', a form of 'folk wisdom', as Hall and O'Shea remind us. In the UK the tabloid press has become the space of formation for a moralizing common-sense, drawing from the historical vernacular of working-class culture and reshaping it to fit with the wider political agendas with which the press is affiliated. By speaking in colloquial words, the tabloids are able to propose emerging norms of popular justice.

Hall draws on his earlier analysis of Thatcher and then Blair, showing how this neoliberal momentum has been built over a considerable period of time, and how key the idea of fairness has been to mobilize popular opinion behind cuts in welfare. This rhetoric has aimed at driving a wedge between so-called 'hard-working families' (often low paid but in work) and those others who are receiving benefits. The appeal to fairness, especially with reference to individual cases, undermines, with a view to displacing, older ideas of universal provision, while at the same time concealing the phenomenon of being 'poor in work' (Joseph Rowntree Foundation, December 2016). Fairness marks out the new dividing lines within the ranks of the out of work and the poor in work, and this serves as an instrument in the process of dismantling welfare. Hall and O'Shea also show how media scapegoating of people on benefits impacts on public opinion, something verified by polls such as YouGov and NatCen. There is a decline in empathy for those on benefits and also a wide margin of error in how people perceive rates of abuse of the social security system. Little attention is ever paid to the nuances and contingencies of being a benefit claimant, the unexpected illness of a child, keeping the mother at home and off work for several months at a time; a teenage girl with mental health problems also prompting a parent to stop work for some duration. These are situations for which only the very wealthy are able to afford the kind of specialist care that allows a parent to maintain a full-time job confident that the child or teenager will be properly looked after. Meanwhile the tabloid media and popular television have the power to win public approval for the transformations of welfare by means of story-making as national morality play, and typically (and for whatever reasons) they have done so by finding people who will agree to expose themselves as conforming to stereotypes about 'scroungers'. The public is led to believe this sector of the undeserving poor is much larger than is the case and that only harsh and punitive sanctions will have any chance of working.

Feminism and New Public Management

> [M]ost feminists did not reject state institutions *simpliciter*. Seeking, rather, to infuse the latter with feminist values, they envisaged a participatory-democratic state that empowered its citizens. The goal accordingly was less to dismantle state institutions than to transform them into agencies that would promote and indeed express, gender values. (Fraser 2013, p. 216)

As neoliberal policies took root, so too was what we might call leadership-feminism rolled out across the institutions, directed towards female employment, employability and entrepreneurship. A full investigation of these processes would require a more extended analysis than is possible in this connection; but we can nevertheless indicate some turning points. Broadly speaking, the state, the public sector and the welfare services have been key employers of women. This has been the case right across the occupational hierarchy from top professionals to care workers and cleaners. This is also one of the reasons why feminists from the mid 1970s in the UK were often mobilized within this terrain, as teachers, social workers, health workers and so on. These fields of work were also the site for various struggles for equal pay and against sexual discrimination, again over many decades. Not just legislation but specific codes of practice and vocabularies were put in place. When government, in the early 1990s, set about reducing what they claimed was a swollen state sector, and when processes of privatization were also introduced alongside the scaling down of the welfare system, this female workforce would be required to implement many of these changes. And so one key question relevant to the current discussion is, who were, and are, the feminist professionals charged with devising and putting into practice these programmes? What happens when the private sector is contracted and able to call the shots? Who are the professional women, for example, who devise projects such as *Because I am a Girl*? In feminist theory there has been a good deal of attention recently expended on the question of co-option, or even complicity and collusion (Fraser 2013; Wilson 2015). Sara Farris has recently shown how in the context of EU integration programmes, migrant women (her case studies are the Netherlands, France and Italy) are pushed into low-skill care-oriented workfare programmes managed and overseen by 'femocrats' (Farris 2017). In other words, these are the women who are employed in public sector programmes which, shaped by second-wave feminism, have provided various support services to disadvantaged women, from asylum seekers to battered wives. The feminist co-option here typically evolves around the deployment of the vocabularies of gender mainstreaming, now significantly adjusted to endorse the various techniques and activities associated with New Public Management. In short, what began as a series of women's equality projects, typically within the social services and public sector and within a broader framework of social democratic ideals, by the mid 1990s had been made subject to the countervailing forces of neoliberalism in the guise of 'modernization' and reform of the public sector. Here there is an emphasis on efficiency, cost-cutting, getting rid of 'red tape', semi-privatization of services to new providers, etc. This ethos of NPM has been subjected to detailed scrutiny by Gruening (2001).[20] It is pivotal to reducing the costs of welfare, for those on the receiving end as claimants, but also for the state welfare apparatus as a whole, including its employees, in a move which could be described as the 'economization of the social' (Brown 2015). New Public Management refers to practices of administration including outsourcing and privatization, de-regulation, internal competition, audit culture, entrepreneurial activity and even 'payment by results'.

There is not a great deal of empirical research so far regarding implementation processes in these female-dominated fields. Janet Newman is an exception, having interviewed women of different ages in public administration, the local state and the voluntary (but state subsidized) sector (Newman 2016, 2017). She describes how they claim to have brought their 'feminist inflected activism' to bear, as their workplaces have undergone the kinds of changes associated with the principles of neoliberalism. These women have worked to 'prefigure alternative rationalities'. Newman's sample includes knowledge workers, social entrepreneurs and managers. She shows how women who had developed their skills through the 1980s were then drafted in to pave the way for privatization programmes such as Comprehensive Competitive Tendering. The interviewees describe how they tried to ensure that various measures such as equal pay would be adhered to, and how this involved a good deal of 'ducking and diving'. Writing also about the women whose job it was to oversee gender workfare programmes during the years of New Labour, Newman sums up their activities as the 'paradoxical alignments of feminism and neoliberal governance' (ibid.). As the language of business pervaded these programmes, many of the women she interviewed became, or were forced to become, self-employed consultants and policy advisers, whose job it was to 'translate their civic values into business rationalities'. A good deal of 'self-work' was required of these subjects, as they had to embody the norms of self-reliance that they were also expected to impart. This takes us right into the heartland of the NPM with its stress on leadership, empowerment and enterprise. There is some attempt to subvert these principles, and a good deal of effort is put into being inventive with the resources at hand, leading Newman to insist overall that these women are by no means simple handmaidens of the new orthodoxy. However, more work would need to be undertaken with younger recruits into these same sectors who may, for example, understand themselves as individualized post-feminist subjects, and already have absorbed the values of self-responsibility, making them more likely to be willing to dispense these values to disadvantaged women.[21]

Kantola and Squires (2012) show, with reference to three case studies, exactly how a shift has taken place from 'state feminism' in public institutions to what they refer to as 'market feminism'. They look to institutional processes and to the changing face of feminist social policy. Feminists working in the public-private sector have had to adapt to 'new forms of governance' as neoliberalism seeks to dismantle the older welfare regime, replacing it with semi- or wholly privatized organizations which must tender for funds competitively and also seek to secure funds from new sources. It is through these processes of privatization that the feminist subjects of NPM were forced to become market-oriented or entrepreneurial in outlook, looking now 'to the market to pursue gender equality' (ibid., p. 383). In effect this meant looking to private foundations to fund projects that were formerly provided for by departments of government or the local state. From being employees, many found themselves subject to privatization and hence outsourced and forced to set up as not-for-profits, which again meant looking far and wide for grants and awards. Inevitably the nature of the feminist agenda undergoes changes as, for example, Non Governmental Organizations (NGOs) have to look to the corporate sector, whose working vocabularies are so different from those within the state bureaucracy. Language undergoes a profound shift – from that of policy, often framed in technical or legal language, to a more nebulous emphasis on empowerment, aspiration, leadership or on being a 'champion of women'. This move to the market requires major adjustment on the part of the feminists working in the NGO sector. NPM is the change-maker *per se*, comprising an assemblage of manuals, mentors, tool-kits and seemingly 'common-sense' advice. This is, as Kantola and Squires argue, an ethos which says that the workforce must 'act like private sector managers' (Kantola and Squires 2012). It is within this wider context that young women also find themselves setting up as self-employed experts or consultants in gender mainstreaming or as gender and diversity experts or indeed as women's lifestyle coaches (see also Hark 2016). By these means there is a 'redirecting of feminist goals' towards the notion of 'expertise' (Kantola and Squires 2012). Kantola and Squires also provide a clear picture of how, alongside these transformations, feminist initiatives were also being shut down, starved of funding or dismantled under the rubric of cuts and budget reductions. These changes marked 'the fall of the femocrat'. Kantola and Squires demonstrate a decisive move where gender mainstreaming has to make 'good business sense' in order to justify its existence. The vocabulary has by this stage undergone a profound, even seismic transformation, and the question is raised as to whether those deploying these vocabularies – e.g. 'making the business case for gender equality' – are *de facto* 'complicit' market feminists, as Nancy Fraser would have it. Further questions arise with the out-sourcing or privatization of services, such as providing training and mentoring for job-seekers. Where in the past this work would have been subject to various requirements and procedures established within the public sector, in cost-cutting exercises standards are frequently lowered, with less well-qualified trainers employed to monitor the job-seeking activity of claimants, for example single mothers.[22] So the question needs to be raised as to how programmes for such recipients are devised? How is welfare reform pursued within administrations where at least some smattering of feminist values had formerly been implemented?

Gender and Anti-Welfarism

At this point we may advance the retrospective proposition that the ideas of post-feminism, which in my own account were attributed to the intersections of gender elements of New Labour doctrine, with dominating currents in media and popular culture, might now be seen as even more hostile to women – and thus even more anti-feminist – than was originally perceived (McRobbie 2008). In the guise of the neoliberal language of choice and empowerment, post-feminist discourses managed to legitimate older sexual inequalities and invoke gender retraditionalization, while also giving birth to new regimes of sexism and gender inequity (McRobbie 2008). Deeply indebted to the idea of a gender meritocracy, the ethos of post-feminism also saw, for example, the demise of access programmes devised to support black and Asian women in favour of purely competitive schemes. There are three points which can be made here. Firstly, that a celebratory focus on phenomena such as 'Alpha Girls' actually deflected attention away from those who were unable, under any circumstances, to access the so-called level playing field of the new meritocracy (Littler 2017). Secondly, perhaps even we feminists, were, now and again, persuaded by some of those voices that celebrated female success, for example in schooling and at university, thus blunting our attentiveness to the sharp rise in the gender pay gap, to the high levels of racism that impacted on young women – including those few who made it to Oxford or Cambridge, only to report some time later on the various forms of abuse they encountered on a daily basis – and to the ongoing reality of sexual violence and the new forms of sexism across the public domain, where, within the logic of neoliberal rationality, inequality is an inevitable and desired outcome. The third and final factor which perhaps inured us to rising inequalities was that, in the UK, the New Labour government did embark on some programmes which were indeed beneficial to women, the most obvious being the Sure Start provision for nursery care for pre-school children. This corresponds with what Stuart Hall labelled New Labour's 'double shuffle', an agenda led by a commitment to neoliberal values but within which was tucked a residual social democratic element (Hall 2003). Of course, this expansion of childcare also contributed directly to what we have been discussing so far, i.e. the way in which work has been prioritized as the preferred mechanism of welfare reform. Overall this heralds a shift away from a 'society against inequality' to a society only nominally against more individualized or 'targeted' ideas of poverty (Zamora 2014). Arguably this cultural groundwork of individualizing poverty is undertaken within the field of media and popular culture. Meanwhile, turning women into workers *per se* is also a way of 'delegitimizing social security' (ibid.). Work is set against welfare rather than in relation to it, a good and necessary thing in times of adversity. The self-respect of contemporary womanhood, no matter how low her level of qualifications, and how adverse her circumstances, requires that she be in the workforce, and this becomes a defining mark of respectability and citizenship. It is what – this is what one presumes George Osborne would have argued – gets her out of bed in the morning.

It is not enough simply to commend working women and deplore those on benefits; instead there is a constant effort to incite a climate of reprobation and judgement. Benefit claiming and welfare 'dependency' find expression in corporeal terms as reprehensible 'lifestyle' choices. That is to say that the intensification of attention to the female body, which has become normalized across the feminine media, is here accentuated to highlight the particular failings of the bodies of poor or unemployed women. A punitive dynamic extends both to the body of the woman and to the details of her personal circumstance and environment. This spotlight of negative attention frequently entails a shaming function.[23] In this way the pernicious nature of welfare reform dovetails with and even collapses into the formulaic vocabularies associated with various other forms of 'feminine' complaint, such as being overweight. Just as women featuring in women's magazines or in television programmes will describe the experience of being body-shamed on being confronted with photographs of themselves showing excess weight, which in turn encouraged them to adopt a weight-loss plan, so also does poverty and benefit-shaming reach down into this repository of personal self-blame, in the hope of pushing the victim towards a more respectable identity. If benefit-shaming can be seen as just another form of drawing attention to personal 'weakness', then the public policy dimension of welfare reform, what Wacquant refers to as 'punishing the poor', is disguised by the regime of visual media governmentality.

The demonization of sections of the working class has a long history. Skeggs reminds us of the nineteenth-century strategies for knowing and classifying the working class through photography, a practice intensified by the perverse erotic gazes of middle-class men, often urban investigators, who took pleasure in the sight of working-class, slum-dwelling women (Skeggs 2012; Walkowitz 1985). Fear, fascination and desire motivated these undertakings. Such activities have been understood as part of the disciplinary panoptical power of the Victorian middle classes, and a similar logic can be seen at play today in the countless documentations, in the press and on television, of working-class and mostly young women, often mothers, in the streets in states of undress and drunkenness, or else in their homes or communities, behaving in ways which invite scorn, contempt or disgust (but also, it seems, lewd fascination) on the part of the viewer. This longer history of contempt, undergirded with fear, was reactivated after a period of dormancy, when in the early 2000s and throughout the times of post-feminism, popular culture became more openly aggressive with regard to encouraging or inciting class hatred, often in ways that were laced with irony, as if this somehow exonerated the protagonists (McRobbie 2008). Eventually, left-wing and radical journalists and academics began to analyse and contest this phenomenon (for example people being labelled as 'chavs') while also ascribing its underlying values to the emergence of a more aggressively neoliberal ethos of competition, hierarchy and symbolic violence. Today's mediated anti-welfarism can also be traced back, not just to the early days of the Cameron Coalition government, and to the statements made by the Prime Minister about his moral mission to reduce the nation's welfare bill, as Lydia Morris demonstrates with precision (Morris 2016), but also, once again, to the ebullient times of New Labour. Peter Mandelson, in his 1997 speech inaugurating the opening of the Social Exclusion Unit, mimics, while also appearing to endorse, the coarse language of the tabloids, when he talks about that section of society who are 'losers' and 'no hopers' and who, adopting the voice of those he berates, 'are perverse in our failure to succeed' (Skeggs 2005, quoting Mandelson 1997).

Skeggs provides the most extensive analysis of the denigration by media of working-class women in 'cartoon' type imagery (ibid.). They are depicted as 'fat' and 'repellent', and their bad habits – including eating unhealthy food and smoking and drinking too much – not only casts a cloud over their capacity as mothers, but also shows them to be almost incapable of self-improvement. Skeggs argues, first, that such portrayals deflect attention away from the substantial reductions in budgets that are allocated by government to welfare;

second, that they signal the fears and anxieties of the middle classes, who see their authority being eroded; and third, that this degraded status marks the economy of value within neoliberalism, wherein individuals are relentlessly pushed to consider themselves as units of human capital. Lacking access to the social and economic capital of their middle-class peers renders these women as valueless, in effect a 'burden on the state'. Skeggs's sociological aim is to restore value and meaning to these women as they are, and to valorize non-'propertized' female relationships such as caring, and creating community. She makes the case for understanding the lives of women in economically adverse circumstances in terms of a working-class culture that somehow refuses to make good, which refuses so many incitements to become productive and to shape up, even though it is constantly told that it would gain the approval of its social betters for at least trying.

This is an important argument from Skeggs: that those who do not comply with the requirement to improve their human capital find themselves open to contempt and indeed abuse, on the basis that they are discounted from circuits of value. What also needs to be foregrounded is the systemic withdrawal of provisions for profoundly disadvantaged persons, often living in areas of historical post-industrial decline. And, likewise, where in more social democratic times the representation of such declining communities in the media might have been framed in terms of compassion and sympathy; for example, showing a strong working-class mother doing her best against the odds for her children; current genres instead appear editorially to look out for 'cases' where a logic of abjection can be pursued. The camera is deployed to this effect, lingering on shots of the unkempt woman who has lost teeth, and who is also overweight and untidy. This denigration of the working-class woman reliant on benefits has been a key element, indeed a weapon, in the ideological justification of an anti-welfare agenda, as if it is all her own fault. This demonization process is also about instilling fear within the ranks of the poor-in-work, compelling them to accept their load unquestioningly, as we see in the case of the army of working-class women now browbeaten into accepting a seemingly long-term future of low-paid and temporary jobs, since this is what, for them, the modern work society looks like.[24] Publicly mediated denigration and symbolic violence in this milieu are dividing practices that have intra-class consequences, while simultaneously firing the flames of prejudice, by providing viewers with a reassurance that even if they aren't doing as well as could be expected, at least they are not like 'them'. Solidarity is undercut by this singling out or shaming of specific families, or even specific mothers, especially when their cases are turned into putatively entertaining stories. (And it is worth noting that even when they are not 'entertaining', they are at least told in such a lurid way as to invoke some sense of disapproval or reprobation.) We have already highlighted what Morris refers to as the 'erosion of public conceptions of desert', and an apparent loss of compassion or empathy on the part of the general public, as consequences of the effort to present welfare dependence as in effect 'immoral' (Morris 2016, p. 101). Although in Morris's account there is no particular focus on the role of the media in the roll out of neoliberalism in the UK, and no specific attention to the way in which women have been addressed within this regime, nevertheless she pinpoints the centrality of morality and the mobilization of a set of fairness discourses in what amounts to something of a war of attrition on the benefit system, 'widening the net of conditionality', pushing levels of entitlements down, and outsourcing to private providers who in turn become 'sanction brokers', ensuring for example that single mothers whose youngest child is five years old will attend sessions to propel them rapidly into paid work. In this context, the punitive system moves from those out of work, to affect also those in work, but who are still reliant on benefits to make ends meet. This marks a threshold, as politicians keen to implement the government's agenda see how far they can push the debate around fairness – can it become immoral to be working but still taking working tax credits or housing benefit? This scenario is what Morris posits as the 'new frontier' (Morris 2016).

The regime of visual media governmentality brings key elements of the apparatus of the state together with media institutions, supplemented by the informal power of social media, to create a new moral economy of gender, which legitimates the further dismantling of social security and the welfare state. What has been highlighted here is the extent to which women now stand at the heart of the new work economy. We have shown how their active participation in the labour market grants them recognition and respectability even when the work they do is low paid, temporary and possibly on zero-hours contracts. Popular ideas of fairness are mobilized to undermine older notions of universal social security, and the media – including social media – become the key purveyors of morality narratives that seek to establish the boundaries of acceptable behaviour. This produces intra-class hostilities that contribute to a wider climate of antagonism and the decline of compassion across the social field. The discourses of contemporary neoliberalism appropriate selectively from liberal feminist ideas about work and careers as the routes to female independence and success. It is thus primarily in the field of economic activity that 'feminist co-option' takes place. Neoliberal values serve to create antagonism between those in work at the lower levels and those who may be their neighbours but are not in work. Overall this recalibrating of social morality, so that the old system of protection gives way to a conditional, targeted and sanction-led provision, offers another instance of labour reform (McRobbie 2015). Even in work women are being driven harder to become less reliant on in-work benefits. This makes their moral status a moving horizon: no sooner has it been acquired than there is a risk of it being forfeited. The point is that various anti-welfarist *dispositifs* have been put in place to lower the threshold of consent to the social security system and to instil fear, anxiety and shame on those who are reliant on its 'benefits', first out of work, but increasingly in-work too. The visual imagery of media shaming certainly requires more in-depth analysis, while questions must also surely be asked about those women who allow themselves to be featured in denigratory ways.[25] But, to sum up, what cannot be disputed is the way in which Britain's national imaginary of welfarism has been eroded and chipped away by the visual imagery of shaming and the mediated distance on which it relies. The effect of what Stuart Hall calls 'media-in-dominance' in this instance is to bring about a personalizing transformation (named and shamed), which in turn secures the new basis of post-welfarism as targeted, conditional and sanction-led. This 'moral landscaping' is also directed at those in low-paid work, for whom work-based benefits, including childcare support, are increasingly tarnished with the slur of dependency (Morris 2016). Calls to popular morality undercut the potential for social solidarity, and paid work is held out to women as the guarantor of self-esteem. By these means neoliberal managerialism co-opts a feminist ethos with regard to the progressive role of work and employment, undermining the various forms of universal social protection that social democrats and socialist-feminists struggled for some decades to achieve. The anti-feminism inscribed within this world of public policy is most pronounced when it is directed towards poor, single mothers who are without a voice and hence less able to respond. Often, they are also too busy doing shift work, while also worrying about their teenage children, out and about on the streets, growing up in urban environments and for whom there are fewer if any youth clubs and social services. To be shamed for being 'on the dole', or to be fearful for one's children who have been left unattended while one is (respectably) at work? That is the question. This is where anti-welfarism and the end of the social wage kicks in, for women who cannot 'buy in services' to keep their children off the streets while they work unsocial hours.

4
'Breaking the Spell of the Welfare State':[1] Gender, Media and Poverty-Shaming

> Beveridge himself recommended council-sponsored holidays for exhausted housewives. This mesh of domestic innovations and pronatalist hopes (all aimed ostensibly at the family but in practice at the mother) was threaded through by the language of 'social citizenship' as the apposite voice of the new post-war national democracy. (Riley 1992, p. 195)

In his writing on Thatcherism, Stuart Hall referred to the 1981 publication from a right-wing think tank titled 'Breaking the Spell of the Welfare State'. This vivid phrase suggests a kind of social magic effect, as if welfare, and the edifices of social democracy which supported it, kept the nation 'spellbound'. It also indicates that this would endure unless drastic action was taken. Could we argue that such drastic action has recently been undertaken, particularly in the years of 2008–2018, by a range of media genres, from tabloid reportage to television comedy, from Reality TV to documentary features? In the pages that follow we will examine the ways in which certain prominent media genres, utilizing a purportedly entertainment mode, have consistently portrayed poor people, and especially women, in derogatory ways, as a drain on the nation's resources and as undeserving of compassion and as unworthy of protection. Within this genre they become bodies that barely matter. We thus see the media working in a biopolitical fashion, with close panoptical attention to bodies and conduct and to visual appearances that are coded as abhorrent. This attention extends to fine details of dress, hair and comportment. To suggest that the media play a role in dismantling the welfare state immediately gives rise to questions of power and determination. From where does authorization for this de-legitimization process issue? What are the relations between government and media at key moments in time, such as in the immediate aftermath of the financial crisis of 2008? Is it too easy to see a kind of right-wing alliance between, on the one hand, a conservative-led Coalition government followed by a fully Conservative government and the openly right-wing press and, on the other, the television channels obligated to provide a balance of perspectives, with this particular programming offering a provocative counterweight to more liberal perspectives spread across the schedules? What kind of political economy underlies this attempt to divest the people of its welfare state?

The relation between government and media – and a related concern with the 'manufacture of consent' – underscores the entire history of media and cultural studies from the mid 1970s onwards. Stuart Hall's writing was pivotal, especially in his key work *Policing the Crisis* of 1978, where he, along with his team, traces the connections between local West Midlands newspaper reporting on a seeming upsurge in black youth crime, in which these minor acts of assault and robbery were labelled 'mugging', and the much wider political crisis of hegemony of the 1970s in Britain (Hall et al. 1978). This media moral panic was drawn on by politicians in an attempt to gain consent for a more directly law and order society, which, in turn, not only laid the groundwork for the Thatcher years that followed but also had the effect of consolidating racial stereotypes and thus driving further wedges of race and ethnicity into British society. This led to a criminalization effect imposed on Britain's black population of the Windrush generation. Hall, at the time of writing, was drawing on neo-Marxist writing of Althusser and Gramsci, which helped him formulate a distinctively historical conjunctural analysis along with a theory of media as an ideological state apparatus operating with 'relative autonomy' and thus with a licensed distance from government and the full powers of the state. My point here in this current undertaking is not to search for a causal relation but instead to show connections and associations, while also taking into account how relations of power and domination themselves change and take new shapes with advances in technology. With the rise of digital media and the internet as a decentralizing force, we witness media fragmentation and de-regulation, as the previous regime of gatekeepers and watchdogs are all but swept away. These changes fit more easily with both Foucault's and Deleuze's focus on microscopic flows of power directed towards bodies and populations, promising freedom and self-regulation. Deleuze, in conversation with Foucault's writing, anticipates a further devolved networked power as 'control of communications', operating by means of modulation (Deleuze 1996).

This chapter takes the form of a series of reflections, where I make an argument about the articulations between the social position of poor women struggling on workfare and the stigmatizing media stereotypes which abound. In brief, the argument is that together these create an incarceration effect: the woman is doubly contained, first in circumstances and in an environment that provides few if any chances for material improvement and, second, by the constraints of being seen in stereotypical terms by others and, as Tyler reports, seeing herself also in these terms and having few resources to break out of this pervasive negative visibility. In what follows, there is, first, a consideration of 'Reality TV as social worker', where I draw on the analysis of Ouellette and Hay (2008). Second, I provide a brief overview of the extensive feminist scholarship on poverty-shaming television genres and on stigma, abjection and poor, white women (Tyler 2013; Jensen 2018).[2] My own focus here is with one such person, the figure of White Dee from the series *Benefits Street*. Third, I offer a commentary on how racism has run through the British welfare state, such that there can be no unambivalent nostalgia for an untainted social democracy. Fourth and finally, I suggest that ideas of protecting vulnerable and disadvantaged sectors of the population have been ideologically swept away, aided by current Reality TV programming, which observes poor people, and especially women, in degrading ways and which seeks to expose and humiliate them into self-improvement by means of employability and by taking on the mantle of self-responsibility. I ask the question as to what forms of care can be nowadays envisaged, and how can anti-racist feminist cultural studies play some role in embarking on such a programme?

Reality TV as Social Worker?

Writing about Reality TV in the United States, Ouellette and Hay propose, provocatively, that as social work and social assistance programmes in the US are run down and eviscerated, their functions are delegated to the various make-over programmes, which, in effect, transpose the American self-help ethos into a televisual format accessible to millions (Ouellette and Hay 2008; see also Williamson and Littler 2018). There is less actual shaming here, more mild humiliation followed by instruction and advice. Ouellette and Hay understand the special power of television to be able to guide people so that they become 'responsibilized'. These are 'strategies of government through self-learning' and television is co-opted into this new realm of civic duty 'at a distance' from government. The remit is to focus on conduct and behaviour delivered in such ways as to avoid ideas of 'entitlement or welfare dependency'. Various different types of experts are brought on board to mentor or tutor the needy or dysfunctional parent so that she becomes a better mother. Ouellette and Hay are here referring to the kinds of programmes often bought by US channels from the UK, such as *Supernanny*. They argue that this role situates television as an 'analytic of government', constantly telling people that they must work on themselves. 'The privatization of the welfare state entrusts pastoral care to the media' (ibid., p. 24). This process is also put in a longer historical trajectory, echoing Rose, reiterating those 'powers of freedom' through which modern government developed ways of inciting the working classes to act and behave in accordance with emerging norms of civic propriety (Rose 1999). A new way of governing is now being devised specifically for the television and entertainment apparatus. While these authors are right to argue that the media formats present a new definition of welfare as self-management, the sheer scale of this transfer of responsibility from state and institutional care and welfare (even in its reduced form) to the commercial spheres of television and entertainment companies needs more historical and empirical fleshing out, in particular with regard to the depletion of the state apparatus and how this actually takes place. We could surmise then, that the vocabulary dominating the television shows casts doubt on the professional codes of practice that have prevailed in the social work departments and in the Job Centres. Public television 'neoliberalizes welfare' through its focus on a cast of characters who comprise a procession of hapless women, fraudsters, cheats and malingerers (Ouellette and Hay 2008). And the implication is that the services of the social worker can be dispensed with when the needy person can be persuaded by a television expert to 'start over' and adjust her lifestyle. This is 'an approach to welfare' that downgrades social workers, child therapists and health workers by removing them from sight in favour of a range of more vaguely defined lifestyle experts who advise on modes of self-responsibilization through 'practical demonstrations of techniques and rules' ranging from healthy eating to good parenting to neighbourliness and so on. Ouellette and Hay provide a strong frame for understanding the dissemination of values that typecast the poor and, in our case poor women, as their own worst enemies and which also push them towards mending their ways. They also help us to better understand how there has been a significant transfer of symbolic power away from the public sector (the 'bureaucratic field' as Wacquant names it) towards the various spaces of media and popular culture (Wacquant 2005). This corresponds to the running down or de-professionalization of those employed within the social institutions; less emphasis on training and on qualifications, more on having an entrepreneurial outlook, and even the introduction of payment by results mechanisms.[3] The television programmes confirm a more adversarial style of instruction, a media pedagogy that would be deemed unacceptably informal and personalized within the state apparatus, where staff must adhere to clearly articulated codes of practice. At the very least we could suggest, then, that the quick-fix styles of expert engagement in Reality TV cast doubt on the bureaucratic regime of social services, housing offices and employment exchanges. While the whole shape and function of social security in the United States is very different from the British welfare state, Ouellette and Hay provide a valuable analysis of how the rise of one media format is concurrent with the decline of state provisions of care and protection. Likewise, the techniques of resilience, mindfulness and self-help have also 'magically' found themselves transplanted into the Job Centres of the UK as a panoply of techniques designed to get so-called depressed people back into work. The dismantling aspects of welfare are also evident in the job losses in these sectors, and in the rise of casual and paid by the hour working contracts among the advisory staff. Overall, the need for traditional social services, and for the sensitive and compassionate treatment of claimants in Job Centres, is undermined by the new common-sense of Reality TV. As Dan Finn also points out, it is not just the reported closure of the Job Centres that reduces humane face-to-face contact between advisers and claimants; it is also that the job losses that accompany these closures, thinning down the employees of the welfare institutions, are made up for by online services, which, as the film *I, Daniel Blake* showed, poses a whole range of problems for vulnerable people (Finn 2018).

Little Britain

As has already been noted by Imogen Tyler, the BBC TV satire show *Little Britain*, first broadcast in 2003 with New Labour still in power, marked a turning point (Tyler 2013). The show's repertoire of welfare-claimant characters included a track-suit wearing, overweight, cigarette-smoking single mum called Vicky Pollard, played in drag by Matt Lucas, and was seen as daring insofar as it breached implicit rules about not exposing poor or disadvantaged persons in undignified or cruel ways (Tyler 2008). The series poked fun at fecklessness, while also pandering to offensive stereotypes already circulating in the right-wing tabloid press about benefits cheats claiming to be ill or disabled in order to receive payments while in fact being able to work, and women getting pregnant to get a place on the council house waiting list. Irony and the apparent fun of being 'politically incorrect', along with a queer-inflected bonhomie, gave the programme its seeming humour, with Tony Blair himself choosing to parody the Vicky Pollard figure in one of his speeches. The time of *Little Britain* introduced the idea that welfare had moved from something that solved social problems to something that created its own pathetic pathologies. This programme could be seen as one of the triggers for media anti-welfarism's ascent into the established mainstream, to become something no longer specifically connected with the overtly right-wing press. Under the guise of satire and being 'edgy', and thus appealing to new, younger audiences, *Little Britain* staked out a claim to the approval of the same increasingly de-politicized demographic that was already under the influence of the Blair ideal of 'the third way'. In this respect we can also chart a continuum of ironic mockery of disadvantaged people – increasingly a staple of everyday life in the UK and a kind of legitimation of disgust – as a 'structure of feeling'. That is to say, dominant social groups discovered such irony to be a relatively new way of reinforcing existing hierarchies by boldly reinstating public expressions of contempt for the 'lower orders' – expressions that previously would have been deemed unacceptable and discriminatory within the times of social democracy. We could say then that poverty-shaming as a device for promoting anti-welfare sentiment operates along this plane of contempt, aversion and abjection and that the modulation effect, which is how Deleuze describes the control of communications, means that its presence ebbs and flows. Poverty-shaming can virtually be made to disappear into more everyday strains of cruelty – normalized or made light of in a context where body-shaming is a staple of women's magazine features about losing weight, and where it is routine that a woman will describe being shamed by her children into losing weight. By this means, poverty-shaming as a device for justifying further reductions in benefits merges with, and is thus likely to be disguised by, apparently more innocuous forms of normative bodily discontent among women.

Abjection

Following on from the tradition of feminist scholarship on class established by Beverley Skeggs, which documented the expressions of anxiety and shame at being deemed 'unrespectable' that was felt by the working-class women whom Skeggs interviewed over a long period of time, Imogen Tyler has provided an account of what she calls 'social abjection' (Tyler 2013). This is a device of contemporary neoliberal governance in the UK, which traverses a great many areas of everyday life, extending to various sectors of the population who are stigmatized, whose claims to citizenship are undermined, who are subject to intensive surveillance and policing, and who are seen as undeserving of any kind of public support. Drawing both on the work of Stuart Hall and Loïc Wacquant, Tyler shows how mass mediated expressions of contempt directed at groups, including welfare claimants, generate over time a 'disgust consensus', so as to, in the manner of what sociologists of moral panic call deviancy amplification spirals, permit forms of governance along the lines of a kind of border control, with symbolic as well as real expulsions helping to consolidate social divisions, reinstate hierarchies and stratifications and justify what Naomi Klein described as 'skeletal social spending' (Klein quoted by Tyler, p. 209). This in turn reflects a wider neoliberal logic of what Lorey calls governmental precarization or, as Tyler puts it, the 'daily production of "social insecurity"' (Tyler 2013; Lorey 2015). From Tyler's case studies of stigmatization at work in contemporary Britain, the most relevant to the current discussion concern the women living in poverty, who came to be typecast during the New Labour years by various demeaning phrases; their homes described in the single pejorative word 'council' and their persons as 'chavs', 'pramface' or 'chav mums', with these terms entering into popular culture as abusive designations for groups of mostly young people whose bodies betrayed the signs of poverty. Some degree of self-conscious levity in the profligate use of these words across the press and television appeared to lighten the weight of the insult and injury, as the screws were being tightened on what was consistently referred to as an over-generous welfare state – one which had apparently removed the incentive to better oneself. If, as Lister argued, the word underclass conveyed an idea of 'conceptual containment', then arguably processes of poverty-shaming in the case of disadvantaged women – women exposed to public view through Reality TV genres – also have this carceral effect, with the streets and the houses in which such women live taking the form almost of enclosures, as if they were quite cut off from other, more respectable neighbourhoods (Lister, quoted in Tyler 2008).

Imogen Tyler also provides the most sustained analysis of social abjection as a regulatory norm evoking feelings of revulsion – the sensation of spitting out something repugnant – in order to return the national 'body' to a state of good health, consolidating those boundaries which mark out those who belong from those who do not. Drawing loosely on Julia Kristeva, Tyler argues that being disgusted by certain types of body is a way of keeping ourselves clean. The nation can confirm its identity by throwing a spotlight on those who deserve their status as outcasts. The low-life other is constitutive of the dominant culture because their presence allows this constant and insistent formulation of who 'we really are', where in reality we are, as Kristeva argues, always strangers to ourselves. It is our own self-estrangement that partly accounts for the need to have these reminders of who we are not, as if to provide some psychic assurance. This is what then provides the seeming desire for the abjection of identifiable 'others'. 'They' live in council estates, they live on 'handouts', they have too many children, etc. These are the 'violent effects of classification'. The sheer repetition of key words and phrases enters into the public lexicon, shorthand phrases, which were once objectionable and that now become normal. Tyler is, however, critical of the standard left-wing journalistic responses to the 'chav' stereotypes that have fuelled this spiralling of class hatred and of poverty-shaming. By opposing this vocabulary by emphasizing the inherent decency of working-class culture and lives, the well-intended left-leaning journalists reinforce a binary, as if to suggest on the part of the maligned working-class that they are not like this. But this merely poses a good working-class identity against a bad one, which does little to explain what is at stake in the construction and circulation of these demeaning images and stereotypes. What needs to be investigated, according to Tyler, is the sustained production of images and narratives, such as those which link poor and vulnerable people with ideas of disgust and revulsion. This repudiation effect is contagious and feeds into wider currents of resentment, hatred and social antagonism. It enflames a climate of everyday violence. Pitching women against women, this day-to-day cultural work on the part of the media appears to create enduring political effects. By these means there is a veritable unstitching of potential feminist solidarities, something which became an identifiable feature of everyday life as portrayed in the popular culture of Britain from 2003, and which has been with us for more than a decade.

It is undoubtedly the case that genres of news reporting in the right-wing press have for many years highlighted women, typically mothers, who as welfare claimants are portrayed as unkempt in appearance and unmotivated to move out of this jobless state – who indeed revel in the free time and income, which can even allow them to go on holiday, or who are willing to tell journalists about the profligate ways in which they spend this 'taxpayers' money', and pose for photographs with their children (or 'brood', as they are frequently referred to), seemingly unbowed and even brazen. More surprising is that this genre of denigratory reporting went almost unnoticed. As these kinds of images then found their way from the pages of the tabloid press into television programmes, it was first and foremost feminist scholars who began to develop the tools and methodologies for analysis of these genres, while also paying attention to female audiences (Skeggs and Wood 2012; Wood and Skeggs (eds) 2011; Allen et al. 2014; Tyler 2013; Jensen 2018). De Benedictis et al. have recently refined this corpus of research by focusing specifically on a newly evolving format which they refer to as Factual Welfare Television. This term demonstrates the central place of the welfare system in this format for television documentaries that also aim to provide a popular entertainment dimension. The best-known and most successful of these programmes was the Reality TV series *Benefits Street*, which drew audiences for Channel 4 of almost five million viewers when it was first broadcast in 2014. The authors provide a valuable analysis of the significance of this new genre of FWT – 'a fascinating reflexive moment within the industry regarding the ethics and economics of popular factual television' (De Benedictis et al. 2017, p. 338). They argue that *Benefits Street* 'do[es] not simply reflect the social world. Rather [it] constitutes it, intervening in the current conjuncture of austerity in powerful ways by shaping public understandings of poverty and welfare' (de Benedictis et al. 2017, p. 352). This attribution of a performative effect derives from the fact that the programme held the attention of so many different groups of people from every level of society for the period of time during which it was broadcast and afterwards. It became a reference point in popular discourse, a touchstone for debate about the benefits system. The aim in what follows is to foreground those features that continue to resonate, and which shed light on the idea of carceral femininity and female confinement brought about by the neoliberal assault on welfare and on the ideals of social democracy. I want to focus on explaining the processes that leave poor and vulnerable populations (in our case women) subject to multiple stigmatization processes. Earlier, I pointed to the way in which the idea of entertainment values, along with the seeming collusion of poor women in these media formats, worked to disguise a more malevolent intent; we can now add to this the way in which the popular mobilization of austerity values, as something ideologically posited as affecting the whole population ('we are all in this together' as George Osborne put it following the financial crisis of 2008), also masked the extent to which this very appeal could be so easily utilized as a further means for 'breaking the spell of the welfare state'. After all, if everyone was being made to feel the pinch, with less money in their pockets thanks to wage freezes, then should not those who avoid work and who are reliant on taxpayers' money also be made to suffer? So, there is a double masking process in place here: the promise of televisual entertainment and audience pleasure, albeit at the expense of unfortunate people who are exposed in their everyday lives and habitus, and the wider insistence that these are austerity times, so that a programme like *Benefits Street* was simply one of many programmes that focused on the fact that the nation had no option but to 'tighten its belt'.

White Dee

Benefits Street took place in the Winson Green area of Handsworth, Birmingham and focused on a group of neighbours, all of whom were reliant for their day-to-day living on welfare payments. The narratives of these lives were held together by the most compelling figure on the street, a woman known to all as White Dee. A single mother of two mixed-race children and a strong character under any circumstances, her participation did indeed lead to offers of work as a local celebrity, and in the afterlife of the programme she took up a number of these opportunities. Ironically, we could say that she filled that space mentioned in Chapter 1 of the lost, strong, working-class woman who in the past occupied a place of dignity, respect and love in the genres of working-class writing and then in television soap operas. However, in modern times such a figure has experienced downward social mobility; indeed, she symbolizes a fate for many who, for whatever reason, lack the resources and the reserves to develop the forms of human capital nowadays required to achieve respectable status in the contemporary polity. But what can we learn, then, from the way in which audiences and academics alike became fixated on the figure of White Dee, and what does she tell us about abjection and poverty-shaming in the anti-welfare climate of Britain in the last decade? *Benefits Street*, for the duration of its five episodes as well as the subsequent debate-style programmes, articulated the tensions and the creeping emergence of counter-hegemonic and resistant elements that Stuart Hall wrote about in the context of the politics of popular culture (Hall 1981/1998). The programme both confirmed and, surprisingly perhaps, fleetingly undermined the anti-welfarist agenda, because of

the leading role played by White Dee, who kept the ratings
high by providing the kind of riveting performances that
make for 'good television'. The programme unleashed high
volumes of hate and antagonism from mainstream and social
media, as the inhabitants of the street in Birmingham were
paraded and exposed as morally deficient characters sharing
in common their status as claimants. But the figure of White
Dee, despite being a single mother and despite being a
smoker and overweight, compelled interest and compassion
as well as fascination. Kim Allen et al. identify different
overlapping readings of the persona of White Dee (Allen
et al. 2014). She epitomizes abjection, as the camera lingers
on her cheap-looking wardrobe, her tattoos, the overflowing
ashtrays and the detritus of the poor neighbourhood where
she lives, including old sofas abandoned on the street. Then
there is a turnaround: for the active role she plays in the
community, she takes on some minor heroic status, and in
this guise there is the narrative expectation that somehow
she will eventually better herself, become someone who
can aim higher. As Allen et al. point out, this suggestion,
expressed by various journalists, confirms Skeggs's argument
that the working-class woman can only accrue value if she
lifts herself into a more elevated social position (Allen et al.
2014, quoting Skeggs). Without such aspiration there is only
the shame of being seen as dependent.[4] The third (and in my
mind slightly less persuasive) reading is that White Dee taps
into a nostalgia for a different time, a pacing of women's lives
not dictated by the frenetic requirements of neoliberalism
to maximize one's assets and economize the self through
various performance indicators. The authors suggest that
the middle-class female viewers might even envy White Dee's
disregard for these expectations in favour of 'maternal time'.
Such viewers betray 'longings' for a society which has not
become defined by the spreadsheets of the present, 'escape
from the surveillance of the cruel and penal neoliberal state'.
Fourth and finally, Allen et al. draw attention to White Dee's
unpaid work in the community in the context of austerity,
where care and social services have been decimated. She
escorts her neighbours to hospital appointments, she advises
on matters relating to benefits. Far, then, from being a fallen-
woman-single-mother, she embodies an active multi-cultural

working-class femininity, protecting her children from racist abuse.

The powerful force of tabloid media-led anti-welfarism, with its repertoire of folk devils, thus struggled in this case to contain the meanings that came into play around the figure of the white working-class female subject. This tallies precisely with the way in which the carceral effect referred to above can never be completely sure that its inmates are totally subdued. The micro-physics of power reveal constant tussles. Nowhere is this more apparent than in the minuscule movements that seek to 'contain' and then recontain the social stereotype. As a figure of female abjection, it is not just that White Dee has to be, in cartoon-style, 'more than in order to be less than', though that device is in place, but rather that the debased subjectivity she conveys is not just a boundary-marking exercise (that 'we' are other than that) but also suggests a moment of normative instability (McRobbie 2005). White Dee actually challenges the shaming effect, albeit outside the frame of the actual series. She later defends herself, referring both to her work record before she became a benefit claimant, and to the fact that she was in a long-term relationship for twelve years prior to becoming a single mother. Here she is both saying 'I'm not like that, I'm not quite one of them' (thereby complying with Tyler's complaint) while at the same time challenging those who see her, and by implication others, in just such terms. Arguably this sets in motion across a variety of mediascapes a chain of further reactions, which begin to challenge and contest the way in which poor women became fair game as scapegoats for the state's abandonment of its disadvantaged populations. White Dee is a devoted mother who, months after the programme had finished airing, declared herself unwilling to pursue a career, despite offers of work, because it would mean not being with her children. She was also attached to location and to the city of Birmingham, with a pride about her class identity. 'I love Handsworth. I am a Birmingham girl and the rougher the better' (Aitkenhead 2014). White Dee picks up on the shaming mechanisms and turns these around by showing herself to be someone who cares about the neighbours whom she also advises. This is not to settle on an image of White Dee as somehow morally exemplary, but rather to point to the slippages that come into play as the device of the stereotype is deployed in the processes of hegemony. There are shard-like openings for alternative accounts to emerge, where someone like White Dee rekindles popular working-class memory, embodying past times of community care and recognition of dependency and vulnerability.

Black Women, 'Welfare Queens' and Anti-Welfare Media

There is incarceration and incarceration. Despite her abject status, White Dee still possesses the privilege of whiteness. Tyler points to the argument that, when shown to be profligate, feckless and unemployable, white people lose the advantages of the racial invisibility normatively ascribed to white people, hence the use of the word white to refer to what previously might have been called the underclass. This is to say that, when they have fallen so low through their own 'bad choices', they come to be known as the white working-class. Stuart Hall argued many years ago that for black people race is the modality by which class relations are lived out (Hall et al. 1978). The former cannot be collapsed into the latter and there is, as we know, an incommensurable gap between the lived experience of black working-class people on the streets of Britain and that of their white counterparts. Middle-class black women are by no means protected from the pervasive and historical force of racism and its constant injuries. This was most manifest in the highly offensive and sexualized comments made about Michelle Obama by a Trump ally and Member of the Buffalo Board of Education, Carl Palladino, not long after Trump's entering the White House.[5] At the other end of the social spectrum the black working class also finds its positionality in the social structure absolutely over-determined by race. In the United Kingdom, the recent exposure of the deportations of members of the Windrush generation – the great majority of whom had worked in Britain, often in the public sector and in particular the NHS, had paid their taxes, and yet found themselves sent back to the Caribbean because of changes in the Nationality Act of 1981 – demonstrates exactly how low-income working-class black people exist within an entirely different category of vulnerability from their white counterparts. This is to emphasize the chasm of difference between white and black working-class people in the UK. Nor are the black middle classes immune from threats of deportation.

White Dee's nickname, apparently bestowed on her to distinguish her from a neighbour Dee Samora, signifies in a matter-of-fact way that she lives in multi-cultural Birmingham. It also conveys how it is a normal and unexceptional thing for white and black working-class people to live alongside each other, experiencing poverty and hardship while also mixing, marrying and having children. Still we might surmise that it is unlikely that a black woman would have agreed to be centre-stage in *Benefits Street*. But neither would they be invited, for fear on the part of television producers about accusations of racism.[6] If black women and entire black communities are constantly prejudged in the context of welfare dependency and so-called irregular family relations, then being in the spotlight of Reality TV could not be perceived as anything other than an intensification of the racializing gaze. To rework Bhabha, the stereotypical white-woman-shamed can display a degree of brazenness; for her, looking back at the viewer indeed is suggestive of certain citizenship entitlements, of belonging, that are not available to the black woman, who in such a moment is immediately caught within the invidiousness of racialized classifications and seen as dangerous, and thus as the epitome of the black other, whose belonging to the national polity is always in question (Bhabha 1986; McRobbie 2005). This is not to say that she has no capacity to unsettle, but that different regimes of knowledge and power are invested in these particular articulations of visibility. Bhabha's racial stereotype does promise some room for manoeuvre, some minuscule space for unfixing the colonizer's gaze, but inequitably so, according to whom it is that is being stereotyped and under what circumstances. Key to Bhabha's argument is that this is also a strategy of knowledge, a means by which the forces of domination try, and try again, to know and pin down and subdue the subjugated other. Because he or she keeps slipping through the net, there is all the more reason to repeat *ad infinitum* what is 'well known' about them. When white women on benefits are shown to be going off on another holiday at the taxpayer's expense, or are sitting among their 'brood' of too many children, the apparently shameless brazenness with which they return the gaze of the viewer or audience, though widely condemned in the media, suggests that they have done no wrong, they have taken from the benefit system what they are entitled to. They are defiantly unrepentant. The black woman is invariably understood as more expansively guilty. The historical legacy of racism imposes itself on the body of the black woman, so that from the start, and from the standpoint of forces of domination, she is potentially criminal, or somehow illegitimate in her status as claimant, while her white counterpart is merely shamed for being on the dole, something from which she can possibly redeem herself by getting a job and improving her appearance (Gilroy 1987). For white women claiming benefits their potentiality for criminality is signalled, but mainly for the reason that Wacquant asserts, which is that welfare itself is being brought closer to the system of criminal justice. For black women such an association has long existed and is merely intensified through various waves of anti-welfare discourse rising to the surface of political debate. Both categories of abject women are therefore subject to surveillance and inspection, but for the white woman the changes to welfare carry some sense that this punitive environment is something new, where for her black counterpart the welfare system always disputed her eligibility. White Dee takes her sense of belonging for granted as a white (Irish extraction) working-class woman coming from a family of trade unionists. This is what makes her 'loud' or 'mouthy'. Her neighbour Dee Samora, who is black, in contrast fears exposure and reportedly criticized White Dee right from the start for agreeing to take part in the programme.

As various critical race scholars have shown, the ideal of respectability, cultivated for the specific reason of the pervasive violence of sexualized racial typecasting, has nonetheless eluded black women, despite their efforts, across the boundaries of social class (Rottenberg 2008). Hazel Carby, in her landmark article of 1987, reminds readers of the history of exclusion of black women regardless of their qualifications from labour markets throughout twentieth-century America (Carby 1987). The indefatigable and remorseless nature of institutionalized racism continues to the present day and spans black women's productive as well as reproductive capacities. Within the departments of the welfare state in the UK, black women have been more intensively policed, subject to surveillance and more overtly castigated than their white counterparts (Lewis 2017). Black female fertility has been subject to more intensive intervention, especially within the realm of teenage pregnancy, and the black female body is subject to wholly different criteria in the lexicon of sexuality and desire (Phoenix 1991). As Shilliam has recently argued, the British welfare state was from the start imbricated with the civilizing project of Empire (Shilliam 2018). It was predicated on a racializing distinction between the deserving and the undeserving poor, the former being implicitly white and male and thus worthy of ascendancy into the ranks of skilled labour, with all the entitlements which were attached to such status, while their wives were, as pointed out in the previous chapter, secured within the framework of the family wage. These arguments have been made with perspicacity by various British black and Asian scholars, including feminist writers such as Avtar Brah, Ann Phoenix and Gail Lewis, throughout the 1980s and 1990s and indeed up until the present day. Black and Asian people were envisaged from the earliest days of welfare as sources of cheap labour, with women locked into low-level domestic work, and often employed well below their existing skill and qualification level. This cheap labour made it possible for the British post-war economy to provide the family wage for the more 'affluent workers' (Goldthorpe and Lockwood 1968).

In such a context it was the Windrush generation who found their way into the post-war reconstruction labour market of urban Britain in the early 1950s, in terms dictated by the Home Office, with women with qualifications in nursing mostly directed towards the NHS and men to public transport, as well as unskilled manual labour. Various writers, activists and artists have over the years described and analysed the exclusions experienced by ethnic minority people in the UK from the goods and services associated with the welfare apparatus, including council houses and access to good schools, as well as to the higher levels of work-related benefits (such as pensions) which accrued to the skilled working-class. In this historical context and, as Stuart Hall and Paul Gilroy have each argued persuasively, the key means by which black people in the UK have encountered the British state have been in policing: this daily reality defines and shapes subsequent encounters with the welfare state apparatus (Hall et al. 1978; Gilroy 1987). Does this, then, not cast a long deep shadow over the purportedly redistributive function of welfare? The answer must be yes. Shilliam has recently made an important contribution to the debate about race and the British welfare system by bringing together the closing days of British imperial domination with the setting up of the welfare state, first in the early years of the twentieth century, and then even more emphatically from the early 1940s. In this latter moment he shows how clear lines of bifurcation were drawn once again between the deserving poor of 'good stock', who were to benefit from the 'national compact', a consensual alliance of state business and labour, and the new undeserving or urban residuum comprising immigrant populations from the Caribbean and from India and Pakistan. The new welfare state developed against the background of this national compact, a reconciliation device providing a social wage, which both militated against white trade union-led class conflict and delivered goods in kind for the purposes of social reproduction and family life. Certain sectors of the workforce not only operated with a closed shop discriminating against recruiting black and Asian workers through an informal colour bar, but also found ways of gaining the wages and entitlements of skilled workers for an unskilled sector, which in turn developed a protectionist ethos, while shunting black and Asian workers into even lower paid sectors of work. The double effects of Beveridge, addressing women citizens 'at home' in the UK, and Moyne, concerned with black women in the Caribbean, was to encourage good housekeeping and maternal citizenship on the part of the former, with the latter encouraged in the Caribbean to adopt the white nuclear family model and, as newly arrived immigrants to the UK, to work in the unskilled sector, often on anti-social hours, with scant political attention paid to the difficulties of their family lives.[7] The national compact was then a racialized undertaking from the start, involving, as Shilliam argues, renewed efforts to introduce categories of deserving and undeserving sectors of the population. Shilliam's writing here demonstrates the value of a longer historical perspective, pointing back as he does to the consistency with which eugenicist ideas were pursued to the detriment of non-white peoples, and the extent to which the welfare state was always imbued with ideas of racial hierarchies and with a racialized division of labour. A key turning point was in the 1970s when de-industrialization kicked in, sending white male workers and their families downwards. They 'sullied' the unmarked status of whiteness as they became undeserving, but a key factor here was that Mrs Thatcher went out of her way to break up the national compact in her struggles to weaken the unions. She claimed the compact was too generous and bred dependency. Showing in one stroke how labour reform was so tightly connected with welfare reform, Shilliam points out how Margaret Thatcher's policies led to an expansion of the category of the undeserving, thus reportedly giving rise to new social problems, such as single mothers and problem families. This was also the point at which the think-tank that provided the title of this chapter through their 1981 pamphlet 'Breaking the Spell' came to the forefront of public debate. Shilliam's work is important, therefore, for tracing the point at which welfare became a target for radical reinvention. There is a long duration here as, over the years, the left falls into line with the right, and as US vocabularies are adopted within the UK political culture there develops a cross-party consensus that post-war welfare was a bad thing that bred dependency. In the US this reached a crescendo with the highly publicized racialized stereotype of the 'welfare queen'. From Clinton in 1996 to Tony Blair (and Schroeder in Germany) social democracy was transformed and hollowed out, shorn of a redistributionist intent, shorn also of the idea that it might compensate for the ills that capitalism had imposed on its workforce (though, as we have seen, this compensation was partial, and predominantly benefited the white working class and white middle classes).

We might now infer that the invidious stereotype of the 'welfare queen' has completely outperformed the hateful work it was intended to do. It has withstood the test of time, remaining a key fixity in the racial imagination, while also insinuating itself into the black female unconscious, establishing its fearful presence alongside the other injurious appellations of racial hatred. Its power and influence hardly need stating. It is simply *the* racist stereotype of the modern black woman. The term in effect inaugurated and presided over – while also firmly racializing – the 'end of welfare' as Bill Clinton envisaged it. While, as we have seen, welfare never really began for black Asian and immigrant populations in the UK, the US 'end of welfare' unquestionably had black people in mind from the start, as Melinda Cooper shows in her account of the right-wing opposition accorded to the War on Poverty programmes established in the 1960s (Cooper 2017). That this anti-welfarism was then over the decades rolled out to sectors of the white population, with, as we have seen, a new regime of white female stereotypes, shows how anti-welfare sentiments have been a defining feature of modern governance from not long after the few short years of post-war 'benevolence'.

Lola Young, writing about the new culture of aspiration loudly advocated during the time of the New Labour government, described the way in which black women's magazines urged the abandonment of too-obvious signs of ethnicity with regard to hair and nails, in favour of a more 'conventionally' groomed body (Young 2000). It is as though the disreputable image of the 'welfare queen' haunts the edges of black female corporeality. More recently, a writer in the *New York Times* reported on how equality gestures on the part of hi-tech employers, which offer subsidized egg freezing procedures, are unequally distributed with regard to race, with black women having to confront various barriers in order to access reproductive technology (Allen 2016). Recent reports from San Francisco also draw attention to how black women's experience of giving birth is likewise shaped by racial prejudice – this follows reports by the tennis star Serena Williams that her symptoms while in the maternity ward were not listened to by hospital staff to the point that she almost died. After all, as Donald J. Trump puts it, 'they' are 'breeders'. The history of racial stereotyping of black women thus forces some revision with regard to the degrees of abjection of the white female working-class body by means of shaming practices. We could suggest a sliding scale of de-humanization. In addition, if the black or ethnic minority woman is not the subject of Reality TV's mockery of the poor, we could go as far as to argue that she is there, invisibilized but present, subliminally, in the guise of whiteness. The white poverty-shamed woman expedites the cuts in welfare that impact disproportionately on black and other ethnic minority populations, often single-parent households, with the mother working long hours or shift work in the low-wage service sector. By these means, forms of visual media governmentality can make use of the prevailing discourses of whiteness, and the possibilities opened up for shaming this sector of the population, to worsen the living conditions of black and other ethnic minority people in the UK. There is, then, hidden value to be accrued from this genre of reporting, and from these television entertainment genres. They do twice the work, by means of a displacement effect. Poor black and ethnic minority women by and large remain voiceless and unrepresented, only coming to notice at times of crisis, such as in the aftermath of the 2011 riots in the UK or, more recently, after the fire at Grenfell Tower in London in July 2017. And as Andrew O'Hagan's subsequent article demonstrated, the great majority of these women are in low-paid work: almost every single one of the women whom he interviewed, as well as those who died in the fire, belonged to this sector of the London workforce. They were mostly employed in local shops and stores, in care services and in health work, part of the global city's service sector (O'Hagan 2018).

Some Brief Conclusions

More attention needs to be paid to how the Reality TV series which trade in the kind of poverty-shaming practices described above get to be made. De Benedictis et al. are seemingly alone in beginning this research, showing in their pioneering article how television producers adopt a range of strategies to defend decisions to make the sort of programmes that focus on claimants and poor people living in areas of high deprivation (de Benedictis et al. 2017). (Typically, according to de Benedictis et al., this takes the form of a handful of television insiders claiming to have themselves grown up on a council estate, of having come from a working-class background, etc.) A key problem for feminist research, however, is that of gaining access to the production processes, focusing on the gatekeepers and editors. It would take something like the study of the BBC's drama department by anthropologist Georgina Born to be able to gauge the factors that motivate the television professionals to create series such as *Council House Crackdown*, and indeed to invent such titles, which repeat and extend the usage of the kind of words that designate and make 'abject' working-class populations (Born 2005).[8] Where anti-racist feminist media and cultural studies scholars have already initiated this work, there is also scope for it to be extended into feminist pedagogy, inside the classroom, where this terrain of study provides a pathway for BAME students and students from working-class backgrounds to develop their own extensive critique, aiming to in some way gain the attention of those inside the media apparatuses. Likewise, when the student body comprises some who will become media professionals themselves, critical debate on the symbolic and real violence of the stereotype also provides them with a vocabulary to challenge the kind of ideas that we have seen implemented in the genre of Factual Welfare Television.

This chapter has sought to undertake something of a summary account, with the aim of bringing together feminist scholars in critical social policy with those working in media and cultural studies. By attempting to show a female incarceration effect, which recent government policies supported by the wide dissemination of harmful media stereotypes have created, I have drawn attention to how the most vulnerable sectors of the population are not just made to suffer, but are increasingly and incrementally deprived of resources which would permit any improvement to their dire circumstances, thus making a mockery of the discourse of self-responsibility and showing the illusory nature of the so-called meritocracy

(Littler 2017). The film *I, Daniel Blake* directed by Ken Loach in 2016 won much admiration for its portrayal of what it means to be unprotected by welfare in contemporary British society. It showed the kind of new punitive regime in place within the Job Centres, staffed by seemingly heartless personnel, who are presumably on payment-by-results commission rates for their successes in getting claimants into work. The film also had the value of opening up to public discussion the dynamics of modern-day poverty, including the demeaning treatment of claimants. Where there might have been a lengthier feminist debate about the white single mother of two mixed-race children who featured in the film, and who turned to sex work as the only reliable way of putting cash in her pocket – prompting an inevitably sentimental sequence where the older male character in the film sought to rescue her from this degrading work – nevertheless as a counter-discourse the film prompted precisely a pedagogic effect for the reason that at the time of its release it was shown up and down the country in a range of community venues including local libraries, prompting animated debate about the workings of the benefit system. However, to begin to undo the triple incarceration effect referred to throughout this chapter would require more radical social change including a widescale poverty alleviation programme. That is to say, poverty alleviation alongside the reinvention of a forward-looking society of care. This would be one which directly countered the historically embedded racializing dynamic of the British welfare state within a reparative frame; it would also mean returning to the question of maternal citizenship to develop a non-stigmatic approach to single parenting. New forms of economic redistribution would need to be invented to reflect changes in the modern work society. Flexible hours, working from home, and reduced working times all free up people, and especially parents and other family members, to be more involved in the upbringing of children in a community environment. Better training opportunities in work as well as day release in further education promises opportunities for widening the qualifications and improving pay through promotion prospects for currently low-paid workers. Health, education and housing would also need to be reimagined accordingly.

While such proposals as these might be seen to suffer either from over-simplification, i.e. in the question of feminist media pedagogy to counter the pervasive popular moralities which accompany the demeaning practices of poverty-shaming, or else excessive utopianism, given the stranglehold of neoliberal thinking in the current polity, and constant recourse to the 'limits of the public purse'; nevertheless, it is precisely these two difficulties that also reveal not just the inexorable weight of current neoliberalism, as if to chant once again there is no alternative, but the seemingly entrenched nature of social polarization. Across the chapters of this short book I have dwelt upon the cultural meaning of social polarization among women and how this is the result of the dividing practices that undergird the 'society of inequality'. This constantly acts to defuse the ethos of the commons, which fuels and sustains feminist campaigns while also constantly resurrecting at a micrological level a whole world of small differences of class, ethnicity and sexuality. If I have dwelt here on the incarceration effect for women, which is the product and outcome of severe material disadvantage, as well as the sustained prevalence of institutionalized racism across the social fabric, it has been to highlight how obstacles continue to be created which reduce the potential for collaboration and 'commoning' across social divisions. As various feminist academics have pointed out, this has meant over a period of twenty years no increase in the number of BAME students – in our case young women in the academy – but also fewer black and Asian women joining the ranks of the profession, fewer white working-class women likewise. This is also the logic of the middle-class neoliberal rationality, which has enveloped and shaped the public system of education. Thus, while it might seem a meagre thing to point to how feminist media and cultural studies can make a difference in the work of countering practices of poverty-shaming,[9] the wider activities would entail finding the means to provide the poverty-shamed populations themselves with these tools and means of communication. This would be to envisage narrowing the chasms of difference which characterize social polarization, and introducing bridge-building programmes to support women out of the incarceration effect. Therefore, as a conclusion, reimagining welfare and conceptualizing a new care ethos might well mean disarticulating from the past and abandoning nostalgic longings for the welfare society of the post-war years, and instead inaugurating a new radical social democracy which provides training for socially valuable care work, which refutes the myth of the meritocracy, and refutes the discriminatory logic of popular moralities in favour of a new era of productive, reproductive and reparative[10] social investment for women and for all.

Notes

Introduction

1   I draw loosely on Foucault and Wendy Brown here, understanding neoliberalism as a form of governmental rationality, which, coming forward to pervade the UK polity in the Thatcher years, applies the rules of the market to the major social institutions of Western capitalist society, urging privatization of state assets (Foucault 2006; Brown 2015). This ethos is also concerned with bodies and populations who are encouraged not just to envisage themselves as human capital but also to develop an entrepreneurial attitude towards the self, which means bolstering personal conduct so as to maximize assets and audit the self with the help of various monitoring devices designed to enhance competitiveness. Neoliberalism sweeps across the terrain previously associated with social democracy, including welfare, organized labour, education and social care sectors, stripping them bare and proposing instead various entrepreneurial, innovation and leadership programmes.

2   I take my lead here regarding the definition of popular culture, rather loosely reworking both Stuart Hall and Raymond Williams, as symbolic practices, which retain vernacular elements of belonging and identity from subordinate social groups, classes and minorities, while at the same time providing fertile ground for the global entertainment and media industries able to extract and leverage maximum value

from seemingly authentic affective and emotional expressions and investments. The formal qualities of popular culture are massified and commodified. Participation is managed and calibrated through algorithmic demographics of audiences, populations, participants, users or consumers. Little remains of potential for struggle, posing new challenges to scholars of 'pop culture'.

3   Aired through February and March 2019.

4   The popular Victorian image of the ideal wife/mother came to be known as the 'angel in the house'. She was expected to be devoted and submissive to her husband, while creating a beautiful home, so that he would have no reason to seek pleasures elsewhere.

5   Here we might point to the increasing privatization of housing and play spaces in the London property market. Attention has been drawn to the phenomenon of the 'poor door' in developments where social tenants are forced to enter the building through an unlit alleyway back door and without the trappings of a well-designed entrance hall. More recently, groups of women have revealed playground rules that bar the children of social tenants from the bigger and well-planned space allocated for the children of those who own properties in these new-build developments.

1 Feminism, the Family and the New Multi-Mediated Maternalism

1   This chapter was first written in 2012 for publication in *New Formations* 2013. Virtually unamended here, it refers to what was at that time the Coalition government in office in the UK. The only changes made to the text include recent bibliographic references in endnotes.

2   See for example *MAMSIE: Studies in the Maternal*, January 2013, 5(1), *Austerity Parenting: Economies of Parent-Citizenship* (eds Tracey Jensen and Imogen Tyler). More recent contributions are referred to in subsequent chapters of this book.

3   Written in 2012, this chapter refers to a moment prior to the quite sudden appearance onto the political stage of a new wave of left-wing activism, including Momentum and the Corbynista movement of mostly young people.

4   David Cameron on BBC Radio 4 *Woman's Hour*, 27 July

2013. See www.BBC/Radio 4/Woman's Hour/ Episode Guide/ July 27 2013.

5 These institutions and organizations speak to and across each other on an almost daily basis; for example, a story in the *Daily Mail* will often be picked up and referred to by the PM in the House of Commons in the following days.

6 Though on the part of Angela Merkel there is resistance to accepting a direct connection with feminism: see www. thetimes.co.uk/tto/news/world/europe/article3756129.ece.

7 See www.bitchmagazine.org/post/re-imagining-revolutionary-road.

8 See the review of the film by Charles Moore, published on 26 January 2009 in *The Daily Telegraph*: https://www. telegraph.co.uk/comment/columnists/charlesmoore/4348788/ Revolutionary-Road-Its-just-snobbery-to-say-the-suburbs-lack-passion.html.

9 From *Four Weddings and a Funeral* (dir. Mike Newell 1994) to *The Diary of Bridget Jones* (dir. Sharon MacGuire 2001) to *Bridesmaids* (dir. Paul Fleig 2011).

10 See the *Daily Mail* online: www.dailymail.co.uk/femail/.../ My-week-man-desert-In-parts-Britain-70-ch. It is also worth noting that in commissioning a British Asian woman to write such an article the newspaper attempts to avoid the accusation of racism.

11 Baroness Ruth Lister of Burtersett, Emeritus Professor of Social Policy at Loughborough University, School of Social Sciences, and author of *Poverty*, Polity, Cambridge, 2004.

12 Patricia Hewitt (then Cabinet Minister) chaired a small feminist meeting at the House of Commons in 2002. Her off-record comments along these lines were made to an audience of about ten, including Bea Campbell and myself.

13 See articles by Imogen Tyler, Kim Allen and Yvette Taylor in *Studies in the Maternal* (2013) as above.

14 See also Segal (ed.) 1983.

15 See Bauman 2001.

16 James 2015, 'Putting Under 3s in Full-time Daycare Can Promote Aggressive Behavior', *Guardian*. See https://www. theguardian.com/lifeandstyle/2005/jan/09/healthandwellbeing.

17 See above note 13; see also Annesley et al. (eds) 2007.

18 For the most insightful recent account of the entanglements of colonial domination and the last gasp of Empire with the establishment of the British welfare state in the early years of the twentieth century, see Shilliam 2018.

19 Mummy blogging moved from a genre that extolled the

daily pleasures and activities of modern motherhood to a more monetized format, in which the blogger is an influencer comparable to a fashion blogger.

20 The titles of magazines from *Just 17, 19, Elle,* to *Good Housekeeping* itself tell us something about this prescribed chronology of women's lives, a temporality subjected to critique for its reiteration of compulsory heterosexuality (Halberstam 2005).

21 See www.youtube/TED.

2 Feminism and the Politics of Resilience

1 By which I mean the organization of the designated female body according to a set of cultural codes and practices and craftings, which over time are constitutive of a gender formation understood widely as other than the designated male counterpart.

2 See also *Financial Times* interview by Jo Ellison with Gwyneth Paltrow, published on 5 January 2019 under the title 'I'm a Real Person', and *UKBusinessInsider*'s day in the life of Melania Edwards, published 19 October 2018.

3 There is a sense that the young women shown in a series of adverts in the *London Evening Standard* (December 2018) for the prestigious Girls Public Day School Trust are somehow 'feminist' on the basis of the strong and confident way in which they look directly at the camera.

4 See James 2015; also Scharff 2012.

5 Gwyneth Paltrow said in her *Financial Times* interview (see note 2) that she competed with herself.

6 See the autobiography of Michelle Obama (2018).

7 Obama describes the warmth and attentiveness of her parents in their modest apartment in Southside Chicago. Her description of her mother as homemaker highlights the invisibility of exemplary maternal black women in the mainstream of women's magazines and popular culture.

8 A white middle-classness that is also energetic, feminine and heterosexual.

9 The perfect life and relationship now extends to lesbian couples, as a television advert aired December 2018 to February 2019 for the new Grandland X Vauxhall car shows. The new model transports the anxious woman to be with her partner, who is in hospital and about to give birth.

10   For example 'day in the life of' features will focus now on academic women, in one case a research scientist pictured at her lab bench (*Stylist*, January 2019).

11   We can be sure that all of these media genres pay for extensive market research to inform editorial directions; so far, however, this is relatively uncharted within academic feminist research.

12   Relevant here is the obstruction of a pop-up event organized to celebrate a book titled *Feminists Don't Wear Pink* at the TopShop store in London Oxford Street, on 6 October 2018. Interestingly, the book was written by Scarlett Curtis, daughter of Richard Curtis, the writer, producer and director of so many British rom-com films.

13   Since writing this chapter there has been a huge amount of media attention to the possible role of Instagram blamed for death by suicide of 14-year-old Molly Russell in October 2018. This has been followed by calls for new legislation to outlaw the availability of self-harm web material.

14   See for example Sarah March, 'Quarter of 14-year-old girls have self-harmed says report', *Guardian*, 29 August 2018.

15   One might refer here to the recent upsurge in young feminist scholars investigating this terrain: see also Ringrose 2007.

16   Curtis 2018; see also note 12.

17   Here we can also point to the role of positive psychology: see Allen and Bull 2018.

18   And indeed, to myself, given the discussion of welfarism in the current volume.

19   One case is the overt class privilege and femininity shown by upper-class television presenter Kirstie Allsopp when she persuades viewers to 'make do and mend'.

20   This also appeals to young women who want to be good girls. They are not defying a parent by going out to clubs when they ought to be doing homework, they are not truanting or getting into trouble at school.

21   Instances of resistance within pop culture are more often found in music, from punk feminism in the 1970s to Fauness today. See also Robin James's argument about how Beyoncé and Lady Gaga merely reiterate the repertoire of the *p-i-r* (James 2015).

22   A dimension of class and race inequality in the politics of feminine readership (McRobbie 1978/1990).

3 Out of Welfare: Women and 'Contraceptive Employment'

1   Some Job Centres have introduced forms of counselling for jobseekers which draw on mindfulness techniques to build confidence and resilience on the part of claimants: see Allegra Stratton, 'Jobless to be offered "talking treatment" to help put Britain back to work', 4 December 2009, available at https://www.theguardian.com/society/2009.

2   One example is the organization that lends out smart clothing to prospective disadvantaged female job-seekers so that they can look business-like and make a good impression, *Smart Works*, which was recently visited by the Duchess of Sussex (10 January 2019). This is not a new initiative but dates back to the years of New Labour and the Dress for Success projects. The not-for-profit ethos suggests the replacement of universal welfare by social enterprise as new philanthropy.

3   See Catherine Rottenberg (2014, 2018).

4   See Mary-Ann Stephenson, *A Female Face*, The Fabian Society Report, 14 February 2019.

5   There has been, for many years and, first of all as an import from daytime Reality TV from the US, a widespread demonization of teenage mothers. Often the format is similar to the US daytime television programme *The Jerry Springer Show*. However, as a more secular society than the US, and also because of a universal system of public health that is also responsible for family planning and thus contraception, the UK has been better able to accomplish the task of reducing the rate of teenage pregnancy; indeed its success has been remarkable. This is a terrain that is also not immune from sensational reporting from a right-wing perspective; see e.g. Sophie Berland and Rosie Taylor, 'Contraceptive Implants Are Being Given to Girls As Young As 12 on the NHS', *MailOnline*, 13 April 2018.

6   See note 9 above, I am referring here to the relatively easy availability of 'morning after' pills, and also to contraception for school-age young women, in some cases through direct recourse to the school nurse.

7   See Polly Toynbee on reports on the drop in teen pregnancy in the UK: 'The drop in teenage pregnancies is the success story of our time', *Guardian*, 13 December 2013, https://www.theguardian.com/commentisfree/2013/dec/13/drop-teenage-pregnancies-success-story-children

8   The link between unemployed women and their seeming desti-
    nation in low-skill, low-pay work was highlighted by Elzabeth
    Wilson (1975).
9   The most salient feature of this pro-family but anti-feminist
    stance is the absence of maternity leave entitlements in the US
    beyond an obligatory three weeks.
10 In the feature film of 2017 directed by Greta Gerwig titled
    Lady Bird, a father, having faced several redundancies,
    pledges the family home in order to raise loans so that his
    daughter can go to a 'good school' in New York, thus inten-
    sifying the pressure on the daughter to do well and become
    successful.
11 Not so, however, in Northern Ireland, where abortion remained
    illegal until 2019.
12 The existence of such powerful groups explains the title of
    Ivanka Trump's recent book *Women Who Work*, as though
    that case has to be made (Trump 2017).
13 George Osborne's speech at Conservative Party conference, 8
    October 2012, quoted in Stuart Hall and Alan O'Shea 2013.
14 This permits fine measures of differentiation, e.g. this kind of
    single mother in comparison to that more feckless kind.
15 Ruth Lister has been the most prominent feminist academic
    and political campaigner to have argued consistently with
    various governments about the age that must be reached by the
    youngest child before a single mother is obligated to apply for
    work; see Lister (2006).
16 Stuart Hall quoting George Osborne, 2012/2013.
17 As Paul Gilroy pointed out in the live art session filmed by
    Isaac Julien for his recent work titled *Capital*, it is as if for
    Harvey there have been no momentous changes to social struc-
    tures over the last decades, just the same old inexorable 'class
    struggle'.
18 For sure, as referred to in the introduction, ideologically
    women are indeed encouraged to be thankful for the progress
    that has been made vis-à-vis their job opportunities; but this
    does not make them, as Streeck implies, a pliant workforce.
19 As Ulrich Beck and Elisabeth Beck-Gernscheim drily noted,
    older women (who have presumably complied with the kind of
    German scenario Streeck applauds) 'face ruin in divorce' (Beck
    and Beck-Gernscheim 2002).
20 My own definition would be that NPM refers to the sweeping
    reforms to many levels of public administration from the late
    1980s onwards that subjected public sector institutions to the
    idea of market forces, thereby introducing not just business

strategies for competition but, in particular, widescale privatization processes. These encouraged an entrepreneurial ethos among 'service providers', who were now expected to set up as independent businesses or even as not-for-profits and then tender for contracts so as to undertake activities previously carried out by employees of state institutions or organizations.

21 See for example Sabine Hark's recent account, which draws on a study of gender studies in German-speaking countries in Europe. Here Hark demonstrates how, as feminism and gender studies gain a place at the academic table, they are also recruited into the transformation of the university as it becomes a provider of skills and competences for the global competitive economy. She refers to gender studies as being tilted towards 'competence training' and inevitably the 'marketability' of gender studies graduates. This means that feminism also becomes a force of change 'from above', or 'part of the action of how we are governed' (Hark 2016).

22 The low level of training provided to outsourced employment agencies such as G4S was apparent in the Reality TV series titled *Benefit Busters* (Channel 4, 2014). There an adviser was shown calling her cohort of job seekers several times throughout the day and deploying a range of seemingly informal strategies, from flirting to cajoling to threatening in a rather dramatic dominatrix style.

23 There is a substantial body of scholarly work on shame; most significant is *Shame and Its Sisters* (Sedgwick and Adams 1995) and *Blush: Faces of Shame* (Probyn 2005).

24 Casualized and even zero-hour contracts also make it difficult, if not impossible, to find time to enrol for evening classes or indeed daytime Lifelong Learning opportunities.

25 It is predominantly women who are foregrounded in these accounts. Further research would need to investigate the terms and conditions upon which women agree to take part in programmes or newspaper features that depict them in demeaning ways.

4 'Breaking the Spell of the Welfare State': Gender, Media and Poverty-Shaming

1 Stuart Hall (1988), referring to a short book titled *Breaking the Spell of the Welfare State* by Maurice North, 1981.

2 Significantly, and as a result of public anger following suicides by participants in Reality TV programmes and accusations made about exploitation by television production companies, these feminist authors i.e. Jensen, Allen et al. were invited to prepare a report for a Public Inquiry on Reality TV (Jensen et al. 2019).

3 This was actually referred to in one Channel 4 Reality TV series titled *Benefit Busters*, which in 2009 tracked the activities of a benefits adviser employed by the outsourced agency and private company A4E to secure claimants jobs, while also providing some rudimentary training in the form of help with the CV and assorted other 'tips'.

4 Though it is also worth noting that in keeping with the lifecycle of the stereotype, as discussed by Bhabha, she will inevitably or invariably fail in her aspirations, she will resort to type, as subsequent media reports duly showed when some time after the series was broadcast White Dee again found herself in financial difficulty and succumbing to ill health.

5 As reported in the *New York Times*, 17 August 2017.

6 *Council House Crackdown* BBC 1 TV, by September 2018 into its fourth series.

7 Gail Lewis reminds readers that from the 1950s onwards many young women came from the Caribbean to work in the UK, leaving their children behind in the care of grandmothers, and so in this sense they arrived as single women. They would typically send money back home, and save for when their children could be brought over to live with them in Britain (Lewis 2017).

8 We might guess that references to the need for ratings and to become a national 'conversation point' would feed into such decisions. Many if not most of these titles are made by independent production companies competing fiercely against each other and hoping to gain further commissions.

9 See note 2 above.

10 By reparative I have in mind new forms of support due to those women who have over the decades worked in low pay, zero hours service sector work and for whom getting to pension age offers little respite. In my own everyday interactions with women like these now in their late fifties and early sixties I hear their channelling of hopes for improvement into the acquiring of exam passes and possible places at university for their daughters.

References

Adkins, L. (1999) 'Community and Economy: A Re-Traditionalization of Gender', *Theory Culture and Society*, 16: 119–39.

Adkins, L. (2016) 'Contingent Labour and the Rewriting of the Sexual Contract', in L. Adkins and M. Dever (eds), *The PostFordist Sexual Contract: Working and Living in Contingency*, pp. 1–28. Palgrave Macmillan, Basingstoke.

Ahmed, S. (2010) *The Promise of Happiness*, Duke University Press, Durham NC.

Ahmed, S. (2012) *On Being Included: Racism and Diversity in Institutional Life*, Duke University Press, Durham NC.

Aitkenhead, D. (2014) 'Deirdre Kelly AKA White Dee: "I Would Never Watch a TV Show Called *Benefits Street*"', *Guardian*, 7 March.

Allen, K. and Bull, A. (2018) 'Following Policy: A Network Ethnography of UK Character Education', *Sociological Research Online*, 23 (2).

Allen, K., Tyler, I. and de Benedictis, S. (2014) 'Thinking with "White Dee"; The Gender Politics of "Austerity"', *Sociological Research Online*, 19 (3/2).

Allen, K. et al. (2019) Reality TV Public Inquiry Evidence, available Lancaster University, http//www.realitytvevidence.wordpress.

Allen, R. (2016) 'Is Egg Freezing for White Women Only?', *New York Times*, 21 May.

Annesley, C. et al. (eds) (2007) *Women and New Labour: Engendering Policy and Politics*, Policy Press, London.

Banet-Weiser, S. (2018) *Empowered: Popular Feminism and Popular Misogyny*, Duke University Press, Durham NC.

Barrett, M. and McIntosh, M. (1982) *The Anti-Social Family*, NLB, London.

Bauman, Z. (2001) *The Individualized Society*, Polity, Cambridge.

Beck, U. (1986) *Risk Society*, Sage, London.

Beck, U. (2013) 'Metamorphosis', Lecture delivered at London School of Economics, January.

Beck, U. and Beck-Gernscheim, E. (2002) *Individualization: Institutionalized Individualism and its Political Consequences*, Sage, London.

Berlant, L. (2008) *The Female Complaint*, Duke University Press, Durham NC.

Berlant, L. (2011) *Cruel Optimism*, Duke University Press, Durham NC.

Bhabha, H. (1986) *The Location of Culture*, Routledge, New York.

Boltanski, L. and Chiapello, E. (2005) *The New Spirit of Capitalism*, Verso, London.

Born, G. (2005) *Uncertain Visions: Birt, Dyke and the Reinvention of the BBC*, Random House, London.

Bourdieu, P. (1976/84) *Distinction: A Social Critique of the Judgement of Taste*, Routledge, London.

Bowlby, R. (1985) *Just Looking: Consumer Culture in Dreiser Gissing and Zola*, Methuen, London.

Bracke, S. (2016) 'Bouncing Back. Vulnerability and Resistance in Times of Resilience', in J. Butler, Z. Gambetti and L. Sabsay (eds), *Vulnerability in Resistance*, Duke University Press, Durham NC.

Brown, B. (2010) *The Gifts of Imperfection: Let Go of Who You Think You're Supposed to Be and Embrace Who You Are*, Hazelden Press, Minneapolis.

Brown, W. (2005) *Edgework: Critical Essays on Knowledge and Power*, Princeton University Press, NJ.

Brown, W. (2015) *Undoing the Demos: Neoliberalism's Stealth Revolution*, MIT Press, MA.

Budgeon, S. (2003) *Choosing a Self: Young Women and the Individualisation of Identity*, Praegar, London.

Bull, A. and Allen, K. (2018) 'Introduction to Sociological Interrogations of the Turn to Character', *Sociological Research Online*, 23(2).

Butler, J. (1997) *The Psychic Life of Power: Theories in Subjection*, Stanford University Press, Palo Alto CA.

Butler, J. (2005) *Giving an Account of the Self*, Fordham University Press, NY.

Carby, H. (1987) *Reconstructing Womanhood*, Oxford University Press, Oxford.

Cooper, M. (2017) *Family Values: Between Neoliberalism and the New Social Conservatism*, MIT Press, Cambridge MA.

Curtis, S. (2018) *Feminists Don't Wear Pink and Other Lies*, Penguin, London.

Davidoff, L. and Hall, C. (2002) *Family Fortunes: Men and Women of the English Middle Class 1780–1850*, Routledge, London.

Davin, A. (1978) 'Imperialism and Motherhood', *History Workshop Journal*, 5 (1): 9–66.

de Benedictis, S. et al. (2017) 'Portraying Poverty: The Economics and Ethics of Factual Welfare Television', *Cultural Sociology*, 11 (3): 337–58.

Deleuze, G. (1996) *Foucault*, University of Minnesota Press, Minneapolis.

Donzelot, J. (1979) *The Policing of Families*, Knopf Doubleday, New York.

Eng, D. and Han, S. (2000) 'A Dialogue on Racial Melancholia', *Psychoanalytic Dialogues*, 10 (4): 667–700.

Farris, S. (2017) *In the Name of Women's Rights: The Rise of Femonationalism*, Duke University Press, Durham NC.

Felski, R. (1995) *The Gender of Modernity*, Oxford University Press, Oxford.

Finn, D. (2018) 'Why are Britain's Job Centres Disappearing?' in *the Conversation*, May 10.

Foucault, M. (1987) *History of Sexuality*, vol. I, Penguin, London.

Foucault, M. (2006) *The Birth of Biopolitics: Lectures at the Collège de France*, Palgrave Macmillan, Basingstoke.

Fraser, N. (2013) *Fortunes of Feminism: From State-Managed Capitalism to Neoliberal Crisis*, Verso, London.

Gill, R. and Orgard, S. (2018) 'The Confidence Cult(ure)' in *Australian Feminist Studies*, 30 (86): 324–44.

Gilroy, P. (1987) *There Ain't No Black in the Union Jack*, Routledge, London.

Goldthorpe, D. and Lockwood, J. (1968) *The Affluent Worker*, Cambridge University Press, Cambridge.

Gruening, G. (2001) 'The Origins and Theoretical Basis of New Public Management', *International Public Management Journal*: 1–25.

Halberstam, J. (2005) *In A Queer Time and Place: Transgender Bodies, Subcultural Lives*, Duke University Press, Durham NC.

Hall, S. (1988) 'Thatcher's Lessons', *Marxism Today*, March, 20–7.

Hall, S. (2003) 'New Labour's Double Shuffle' in *Soundings*, 24: 10–24, Lawrence and Wishart, London.

Hall, S. (2011) 'The Neo-Liberal Revolution', *Cultural Studies* 25 (6): 705–28.

Hall, S. and O'Shea, A. (2013) 'Common-Sense Neoliberalism', *Soundings*, 55: 9–25, Lawrence and Wishart, London.

Hall, S. et al. (1978) *Policing the Crisis: Mugging, the State and Law and Order*, Palgrave Macmillan, Basingstoke.

Hark, S. (2016) 'Contending Directions: Gender Studies in the Entrepreneurial University', *Women's Studies International Forum*, 54.

Harvey, D. (2005) *A Brief History of Neoliberalism*, Oxford University Press, Oxford.

Higginbotham, Brook E. (1994) *Righteous Discontent: The Women's Movement in the Black Baptist Church, 1880–1970*, Harvard University Press, MA.

Hoggart, R. (1957) *The Uses of Literacy*, Penguin, Harmondsworth.

James, R. (2015) *Resilience and Melancholy: Pop Music, Feminism, Neoliberalism*, Zero Books, Hants.

Jensen, T. (2018) *Parenting the Crisis: The Cultural Politics of Parent-Blame*, Policy Press, Bristol.

Jensen, T. and Tyler, I. (2013) '"Austerity Parenting": New Economies of Parent Citizenship', *Mamsie: Studies in the Maternal*, 4(2).

Jensen, T. and Tyler, I. (2015) '"Benefit Broods": The Cultural and Political Crafting of Anti-Welfare Common-sense', *Critical Social Policy*, 35(4): 470–91.

Kanai, A. (2017) 'Beyond Repudiation: The Affective Instrumentalisation of Femininity in Girlfriendly Space', *Australia Feminist Studies*, 32 (93): 240–58.

Kanai, A. (2018) 'Between the Perfect and the Problematic: Everyday Femininities, Popular Feminism, and the Negotiation of Intersectionality', *Cultural Studies*, DOI: 10.1080/09502386.2018.1559869.

Kantola, J. and Squires, J. (2012) 'From State Feminism to Market Feminism', *International Political Science Review*, 33 (4): 382–400.

Lewis, G. (2017) 'Questions of Presence', *Feminist Review*, 117.

Lister, R. (2006) 'Children (But Not Women) First: New Labour, Child Welfare and Gender', *Critical Social Policy*, 26 (2): 315–55.

Littler, L. (2013) 'The Rise of the "Yummy Mummy": Popular Conservatism and the Neoliberal Maternal in Contemporary British Culture', *Communication, Culture and Critique*, 6: 227–43.

Littler, J. (2017) *Against Meritocracy*, Routledge, London.

Lorey, I. (2015) *States of Insecurity*, Verso, London.

McRobbie, A. (2005) *The Uses of Cultural Studies*, Sage, London.

McRobbie, A. (2008) *The Aftermath of Feminism: Gender, Culture and Social Change*, Sage, London.

McRobbie, A. (2013) 'Feminism, the Family and the New "Mediated" Maternalism', *New Formations*, 8: 119–37.

McRobbie, A. (2015) *Be Creative: Making a Living in the New Culture Industries*, Polity, Cambridge

Morris, L. (2016) 'The Moral Economy of Austerity; Analysing UK Welfare Reform', *British Journal of Sociology*, 67 (1): 97–116.

Mukherjee, R. and Banet-Weiser, S. (2012) *Commodity Activism in Neoliberal Times*, New York University Press, New York.

Newman, J. (2015) 'Governing the Present: Activism, Neoliberalism, and the Problem of Power and Consent', *Critical Policy Studies*, 20.

Newman, J. (2016) 'Space of Power: Feminism, Neoliberalism and Gendered Labour', *Social Politics*, 20 (2): 200–22.

Newman, J. (2017) 'The Politics of Expertise: Neoliberal Governance and the Practices of Politics', in V. Higgins and W. Larner (eds), *Assembling Neoliberalism: Experts, Practices, Subjects*, Palgrave Macmillan, New York.

North, M. (1981) 'Breaking the Spell of the Welfare State', The Social Affairs Unit, London.

Obama, M. (2018) *Becoming*, Vintage, New York.

O'Hagan, A. (2018) 'The Tower', *London Review of Books*, 7 June.

Ouellette, L. and Hay, J. (2008) *Better Living Through Reality TV: Television and Post Welfare Citizenship*, Blackwell, Maldon MA.

Phillips, A. (2015) 'On Self Beratement', *London Review of Books*, 19 March, 13015.

Phoenix, A. (1991) *Young Mothers?*, Routledge, London.

Probyn, E. (2005) *Blush: Faces of Shame*, University of Minnesota Press, Minneapolis.

Puar, J. (2012) *Terrorist Assemblages*, Duke University Press, Durham NC.

Riley, D. (1986) *The War in the Nursery*, Virago, London.

Riley, D. (1992) 'Citizenship and the Welfare State' in J. Allen, et al. (eds), *Political and Economic Forms of Modernity*. Polity, Cambridge, pp. 179–229.

Ringrose, J. (2007) 'Successful Girls? Complicating Post-Feminist Neoliberal Discourses of Educational Achievement and Gender Equality', *Journal of Gender and Education*, 19: 471–89.

Riviere, J. (1926/86) 'Femininity as Masquerade' in V. Burgin, J. Donald and C. Kaplan (eds), *Formations of Fantasy*, Routledge, London.

Rose, J. (1986) *Sexuality in the Field of Vision*, Verso, London.

Rose, N. (1999) *The Powers of Freedom: Reframing Political Thought*, Cambridge University Press, Cambridge.

Rose, N. and Lentzos, P. (2016) 'Making Us Resilient, Responsible Citizens for Uncertain Times' in S. Trnka, S. and C. Trundle (eds), *Competing Responsibilities*, Duke University Press, Durham NC.

Rottenberg, C. (2008) *Performing Americanness: Race, Class, and Gender in Modern African-American and Jewish-American Literature*, University Press of New England, NH.

Rottenberg, C. (2014) 'The Rise of Neoliberal Feminism', *Cultural Studies*, 28 (3): 418–37.

Rottenberg, C. (2018) *The Rise of Neoliberal Feminism*, Oxford University Press, Oxford.

Rowntree, Joseph. Foundation (2016) *Monitoring Poverty and Social Exclusion*, Joseph Rowntree Foundation.

Sandberg, S. (2012) *Lean In: Women, Work and the Will to Lead*, Knopf, New York.

Scharff, C. (2012) *Repudiating Feminism: Young Women in a Neoliberal World*, Routledge, London.

Sedgwick, P. and Adams, J. (1995) *Shame and Its Sisters*, Duke University Press, Durham NC.

Segal, L. (ed.) (1983) *What Is To Be Done About the Family?* Penguin Books, Harmondsworth.

Shilliam, R. (2018) *Race and the Undeserving Poor*, Agenda Publishing, Newcastle UK.

Skeggs, B. (1997) *Formations of Class and Gender: Becoming Respectable*, Sage, London.

Skeggs, B. (2005) 'The Making of Class and Gender Through Visualising Moral Subject Formation' in *Sociology*, 39: 965–82.

Skeggs, B. (2012) 'Imagining Personhood Differently: Person Value and Autonomist Working-Class Values', *The Sociological Review*, 59 (3): 496–513.

Skeggs, B. and Wood, H. (2012) *Reality Television and Class*, BFI Books, London.

Steedman, C. (1986) *Landscape for a Good Woman*, Virago, London.

Streeck, W. (2016) *How Will Capitalism End? Essays on a Failing System*, Verso, London.

Trump, I. (2017) *Women Who Work: Rewriting the Rules for Success*, Penguin, New York.

Tyler, I. (2008) 'Chav Mum, Chav Scum: Class Disgust in Contemporary Britain', *Feminist Media Studies*, 8 (2): 1–34.

Tyler, I. (2011) 'Pregnant Beauty: Maternal Femininity under Neoliberalism' in R. Gill and C. Scharff (eds), *New Femininities*, Palgrave Macmillan, Basingstoke.

Tyler, I. (2013) *Revolting Subjects: Social Abjection and Resistance in Neoliberal Britain*, Zed Books, London.

Virdee, S. (2019) 'Racialised Capitalism: An Account of Its Contested Origins and Consolidation', *Sociological Review*, January, 67 (1): 3–27.

Wacquant, L. (2005) *Punishing the Poor: The Neoliberal Government of Social Insecurity*, Duke University Press, Durham NC.

Walkowitz, J. (1985) *City of Dreadful Delight*, Oxford University Press, Oxford.

Weldon, F. (1971) *Down Among the Women*, Virago, London.

Williams, R. (1960) 'The Magic System', *New Left Review,* 1/4, July–August.

Williamson, M. and Littler, J. (2018) 'Rich TV Poor TV: Work, Leisure and the Construction of Deserved Inequality in Contemporary Britain' in J. Deery and A. Press (eds), *Media and Class*, Routledge, New York.

Wilson, E. (1975) *Women and the Welfare State*, Virago, London.

Wilson, K. (2015) 'Towards a Radical Reappropriation: Gender Development and Neoliberal Feminism', *Development and Change*, 46 (4).

Wood, H. and Skeggs, B. (eds) (2011) *Reality TV and Class*. BFI, London.

Young, L. (2000) 'How Do We Look? Unfixing the Singular Black (Female) Subject', in P. Gilroy, L. Grossberg and A. McRobbie (eds), *Without Guarantees: In Honour of Stuart Hall*, Verso, London.

Zamora, D. (2014) 'Can we Criticize Foucault?' *The Jacobin Magazine*, https//:wwwjacobinmag.com/author/daniel-zamora.

Index

welfare as failure of 82
women's magazines and 66
feminism
  anti-racist 102
  consumerism 7, 8, 73
  cultural studies 102
  family break-ups and 78
  female individualism 43
  liberal to neoliberal 12–16,
    97
  mainstreaming 42–4
  Marxist 23–4
  media studies 121–3
  meritocracy 43–4
  mothers and poverty 23–4
  neoliberal leadership 62
  neoliberal practices and 1
  new form of 69
  New Public Management and
    87–91
  p-i-r 7–8, 44–7, 61
  political alignments 13–16
  post-feminism 91–2
  psycho-analytical 8
  repudiation of 68
  Revolutionary Road and
    16–20
  state to market 90–1
  two Marxists argue against
    82–4
Feminists Don't Wear Pink
  (Curtis) 58–9
Finn, Dan 104
Foucault, Michel
  biopolitics 30, 60, 75–6
  conduct of conduct 74–5
  family management 28
  flows of power 100–1
  governmentality 34
  human capital 17, 30
  welfare economy 73
France, migrant women and 88
Fraser, Nancy 13, 87, 91
Freud, Emma 59

Freud, Sigmund 64
Friedan, Betty 40
  The Feminine Mystique 18

*Gender Economics as Smart
  Economics* programme
  76
German Ordoliberals 30
The Gifts of Imperfection
  (Brown) 54–6
Gill, R. 61–2
Gilroy, Paul 117
Girls (television) 45
Giving an Account of Oneself
  (Butler) 69–72
Gramsci, Antonio 85, 100
Grazia magazine 15, 51
Grenfell Tower fire 120
Gruening, G. 88
The Guardian newspaper 15,
  37

Hall, Catherine 28
Hall, Stuart 4, 82
  age of affluence 83
  'Breaking the Spell of the
    Welfare State' 99–100
  class and race 113
  'common-sense of
    neoliberalism' 81
  converging ideologies 61
  'disgust consensus' 106
  ground level political
    economy 9
  Labour's double shuffle 92
  media-in-dominance 97
  middle-class and
    neoliberalism 12
  neo-Marxist culture studies
    85–7
  police and race 117
  Policing the Crisis 100
  resistance to popular culture
    110